Gordon Choi's Analytics Book

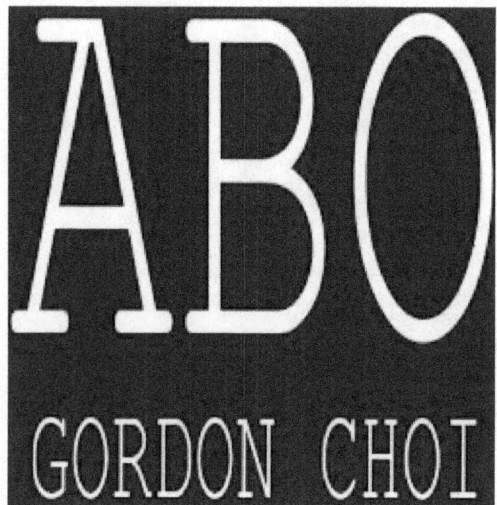

Preface

My book is called "Analytics Book" and has been made available online on www.analyticsbook.org since August 2016.

I have practically reviewed and/or implemented 100+ Google Analytics accounts and/or open source analytics accounts. I truly believe the knowledge of analytics (i.e. Web Analytics & Mobile App Analytics) and its materials need to be made more accessible to the public world through the Internet. The objective of this book is to share my many years of experience and knowledge on analytics (i.e. Web Analytics & Mobile App Analytics) to people who are interested to learn it and/or to use it for academic purposes.

My book has been placed on a Creative Commons license. This license allows you to share the content of this book under non-commercial use.

About the Analytics Book

The book focuses on several topics:

- Analytics - Web Analytics & Mobile Web Analytics
- Google Analytics - Many practical examples of analytics have been demonstrated through the use of Google Analytics
- Open Source Analytics - Get your analytics knowledge up a notch by practically implementing open source analytics tools
- Web Server Log Analytics - The ancestor of website's analytics
- The Common Definitions of Analytics Metrics & Dimensions
- Getting the Skills to become an Analyst

Table of Contents

Mobile Apps

The Analytics Book mobile app is available for download (in Android format).

About Gordon Choi (Analytics Book's Author)

The *Analytics Book* has been solely written by *Gordon Choi*.

Gordon Choi is also the author of *The China Mobile SEO Book* - A book which has been recommended by more than 20 Internet industry experts.

Gordon has developed and founded *Folks Analytics*, a full stack analytics tool for websites, iOS apps & Android apps.

Gordon Choi's Analytics Book has been available since August 2016 and is proudly powered by Folks Analytics. This book is also available in Chinese (CN | HK).

Analytics

Chapter 01

More than 64% of all the websites in the world are currently using at least one web analytics tools. Of the websites that have any web analytics tools, more than 82% of them use Google Analytics. Reference:

- http://w3techs.com/technologies/overview/traffic_analysis/all

Web Analytics & Mobile App Analytics

Analytics Tools include web analytics and mobile app analytics.

Web Analytics - Tracks websites' data.

Mobile App Analytics - Tracks mobile apps' data (including iOS apps, Android apps and sometimes more).

This is the Big List of 200+ analytics tools which are currently available in the world.

Web Analytics Examples:

- Google Analytics (Global, Free & Paid) - https://www.google.com/analytics
- Adobe Analytics (Global, Paid)
- Piwik (Global, Open Source) - https://piwik.org
- Open Web Analytics (Global, Open Source) - http://www.openwebanalytics.com/
- Baidu Tongji (China, Free)
- CNZZ Tongji (China, Free)
- 99Click (China, Paid)
- Growing IO (China, Paid)
- Zhuge IO (China, Paid)

Mobile App Analytics Examples:

- Google Analytics (Global, Free & Paid)
- Piwik (Global, Open Source)
- App Annie (Global, Paid)
- AppsFlyer (Global, Paid)
- Talking Data (China, Paid)
- Umeng (China, Paid)

Analytics: Free, Paid, Open Source, Local & Global

Different analytics tools are different.

Free - Some analytics tools (e.g. Google Analytics) is free to use without any cost.

Paid - Some analytics tools (e.g. Adobe Analytics) must be paid to use. Some vendors have developed the paid analytics tools for commercial use, and provide services to businesses who use the paid analytics tools.

Open source - Some analytics tools (i.e. Piwik) were developed by an online community of developers. They have made the analytics tools and the source codes available for free. However to use it, you will have to do it all by yourself: Install the web analytics, setup the web servers (or cloud solutions), and create and backup the database.

Local (e.g. China) - Some analytics tools (e.g. Baidu Tongji) were developed and are suitable for some specific markets / countries.

Global - Some analytics tools (e.g. Google Analytics) are universal and suit all the markets in the world.

Analytics Tools

Google Analytics

Google Analytics is the mostly used web analytics tool in the world.

- Google Analytics provides both web analytics and mobile app analytics for free. It also has a paid version, Google Analytics Premium.
- With web analytics, it tracks websites' data through using a JavaScript-based tracking code which must be added to each web page.
- With mobile app analytics, it tracks both iOS apps (with the iOS SDK) and Android apps (with the Android SDK). SDKs must be implemented into the mobile apps.

When you are using the free version of Google Analytics for your website, your data are sent to and store in Google's servers. This means you are not require to take care of the storage of your data. Google Analytics can process your data into reports very quickly (or in some cases quite immediately).

You have no control on how to store your data with the free version, so often you may get reports with sampled data. Having a large amount of sampled data in your reports can hinder the ability of your detailed data analysis.

Piwik

Piwik is an open source analytics platform and is a free software. Piwik started as only a web analytics tool, but subsequently has also become a mobile analytics tool with SDKs available for iOS apps and Android apps.

The upside of Piwik is:

- You will be able to store your website's full data in the machine (or cloud solution) of your choice.

The downside of Piwik is:

- You will have to do-it-yourself (DIY) when installing Piwik, setting up and backing up Piwik's database, and setting up and managing the web server (and/or cloud solution) that is running your Piwik setup.

Open Web Analytics

Open Web Analytics (OWA) is another open source web analytics tool which is similar to Piwik.

Adobe Analytics

Adobe Analytics was originally Omniture Site Catalyst. It is a very powerful web analytics tool which has been developed for commercial use.

Complicated tracking setup is available for your websites from Adobe Analytics. The proper setup will definitely require the expertise of Adobe's implementation engineers to take you through the design and implementation of the entire tracking solution process.

Baidu Tongji

Baidu Tongji is Chinese search engine Baidu's version of web analytics tool. Baidu Tongji has made basic reports available which include your website's sessions, page views, conversions (if you have it setup), etc. It lacks advanced features/reports such as advanced segmentation, custom reports, custom dimensions and metrics, calculated metrics, etc.

Baidu provides two versions of Baidu Tongji.

- The first version is available only to Baidu's advertisers who have paid search accounts. By default, Baidu's paid search data has been made available in this version. If you're a Baidu paid search advertiser, make sure you log onto the correct version of Baidu Tongji account.

- The second version is available to anyone who has registered Baidu Tongji through a typical Baidu account (which is free). No Baidu paid search data/report is available in this version.

The user interface of Baidu Tongji is only in Simplified Chinese language.

Next Chapters

Gordon Choi's Analytics Book *has been available since August 2016 and is proudly powered by* ***Folks Analytics***.

Web Analytics vs. Mobile App Analytics

Chapter 02

Analytics Tools include web analytics and mobile app analytics.

- Web Analytics works on websites, uses JavaScript-based tracking codes to collect data, and identifies unique users with cookies.
- Mobile app analytics works on apps (that run on mobile or tablet devices), uses SDKs to collect data, and identifies unique users with IDs (IDFA for iOS and/or AID for Android).

This is the Big List of 200+ analytics tools which are currently available in the world.

Websites

Web pages are coded mainly in HTML/CSS/JavaScript.

- HTML defines the structure (or layout) of the pages.
- CSS provides the look-and-feel of the pages.
- JavaScript defines how users can interact with the pages.

Of course, most websites have to communicate with the backend (i.e. databases), and the codes may be written in PHP, Python, Java, Ruby, Asp.Net, etc. We aren't going to cover this topic.

Web Analytics Tools

The major objective of web analytics tools is to track data on websites.

Depending on the specific web analytics tool that you are using, usually a JavaScript based tracking code must be placed on each page of your website. When the tracking code has been implemented, the web analytics tool starts to track the data.

Scope of Web Analytics

Web analytics tools have been developed to solely track data for websites, whether the websites are optimized for desktop screens or mobile screens.

```
User -> Desktop -> Web Browser -> Website (Optimized for Desktop or Tablet)
-> JavaScript-based Tracking Code -> Data Collection -> Data Processing ->
Data Reports Appears in Web Analytics ToolsUser -> Mobile -> Web Browser
-> Website (Optimized for Mobile) -> JavaScript-based Tracking Code -> Data
Collection -> Data Processing -> Data Reports Appears in Web Analytics Tools
```

How Websites Identify Unique Users

Websites identify unique users with cookies.

Cookies have been used on websites for many years. Cookies enables users to perform certain actions on websites. For example, the first time a user visits a ecommerce website and places an item in the shopping cart, but hasn't completed the entire transaction. A cookie has been placed on this user's web browser (e.g. Chrome) in order to remember him/her (and the item he/she places in the shopping cart). The second time the same user comes back to the ecommerce website and browses to his/her shopping cart. He/she sees his/her item in the shopping cart and continue to complete the transaction. Without a cookie, the website would not have been able to remember the shopping cart item for the user.

For web analytics tools, cookies are placed on users' web browsers. During subsequent visits of the same user to the website, the website will remember the user is the same person (cookie).

Below is an example of how the web browser cookie looks like.

```
HTTP/1.1 200 OKSet-Cookie: AHSID=AARONmxn67; Domain=example.com; Path=/;
Expires=Wed, 13 Nov 2018 15:18:00 GMT; Secure; HttpOnly
```

The cookie's name is AHSID, and its value is AARONmxn67.

Issues of Using Cookies to Identify Unique Users

The cookies which were previously stored on the web browsers won't work for identifying unique users when:

- A user switches to a different web browser (e.g. Firefox) from the web browser (e.g. Chrome) he/she was visiting your website last time.
- A user switches to a new desktop computer and from this new desktop computer he/she visits your website.
- A user visited your website through his/her desktop computer, but this time he/she visits your website from his/her mobile phone's web browser.
- A user deletes cookies from his/her web browsers before he/she visits your website.

Mobile Apps

In mobile apps, the "pages" you can see aren't actually web pages that are coded in HTML/CSS/JavaScript. The pages on a mobile app is known as screens.

For example, an iPhone runs the iOS operating system. Mobile apps running on iPhones (and/or iPads) are coded mainly in Objective-C and/or Swift.

For example, an Android phone runs the Android operating system. Mobile apps running on Androids are coded mainly in Java.

Mobile App Analytics Tools

The major objective of mobile app analytics tools is to track data on mobile apps.

Depending on the specific mobile app analytics tool that you are using, usually a SDK (software development kit) must be implemented on your mobile app. When the SDK has been implemented, the mobile app analytics tool starts to track the data.

Note that mobile phones from different vendors are installed with different operating systems that are incompatible to one another. SDKs are operating system dependent.

- An iOS SDK must be developed to specifically install and track data on mobile phones (i.e. iPhones) which are running the iOS operatin system.
- An Android SDK must be developed to specifically install and track data on mobile phones (i.e. Android phones) which are running the Android operating system.
- Other SDK must be developed to specifically install and track on mobile phones which are running other operating systems. Note, we aren't going cover the topics of mobile phones and operating systems other than iPhones / iOS and Android phones / Android operating system.

Scope of Mobile App Analytics

Mobile app analytics tools have been developed to solely track data for mobile apps, whether the apps are installed on iPhone/iPad (i.e. iOS) or Android. Note, we aren't going to discuss mobile app analytics tools for mobile operating systems other than iOS and Android.

```
User -> Mobile -> iOS App -> SDK (for iOS) -> Data Collection -> Data Processing
-> Data Reports Appears in Mobile App Analytics ToolsUser -> Mobile -> Android
App -> SDK (for Android) -> Data Collection -> Data Processing -> Data Reports
Appears in Mobile App Analytics Tools
```

How Mobile Apps Identify Unique Users

Mobile apps identify unique users with some unique device / operating system IDs.

iOS uses IDFAs (Identifier for Advertisers) to identify unique iPhone (and/or iPad) users. An IDFA is a 32-digit string in which the format is 8-4-4-4-12. Example of an IDFA:

```
6D92078A-8246-4BA4-AE5B-76104861E7DC
```

Android uses AIDs (Advertising IDs) to identity unique Android phone users. An AID is a 32-digit string in which the format is 8-4-4-4-12. Example of an AID:

Issues of Using IDFAs and AIDs to Identify Unique Users

IDFAs and AIDs have some issues when they are used for identifying unique users on iPhones and Android phones respectively.

- IDFAs can be reset by iPhone (and/or iPad) users, An AIDs can be reset by Android phone users.
- After re-installing the operating system on your phone, the IDFAs and/or AIDs are reset.

Why Identifying Unique Users is Important?

On websites, you identify unique users with cookies. On mobile apps, you identify unique users with IDFAs and/or AIDs depending on the type of phones and/or operating systems.

The reason behind this is for in-depth data analysis of your users, you will want to build the click stream (or even the conversion funnel) of each user.

Previous Chapters

- Chapter 01 - Analytics

Next Chapters

- Chapter 03 - Google Analytics
- Chapter 04 - Google Analytics Tracking Codes
- Chapter 05 - Google Analytics Traffic Sources

Gordon Choi's Analytics Book has been available since August 2016 and is proudly powered by Folks Analytics.

Google Analytics

Chapter 03

Google Analytics is a free and an extremely powerful tool for you to monitor your website's data.

Tracking Method

Google Analytics provides JavaScript based tracking code in which you are required to install on your website. This will then enable Google Analytics to collect data from your website.

For Google Analytics to work properly, the minimum requirement is the tracking code must be installed on all the web pages of your website.

Cost

Google Analytics is free to use. The exception is if you are using the paid version, Google Analytics Premium.

Features

The types of and the number of reports that are available have exceeded most (if not yet all) free and paid web analytics tools. Just to name a few:

- You are shown reports based on your website users' origin of locations (i.e. Countries, regions or cities).
- You can find out your users' device types (i.e. mobile, desktop or tablet) and the device names when they visited your site.
- You can find reports regarding your site users' traffic channels and sources.
- You can find reports on all your web pages and the landing pages.

- You can look at your reports by applying Advanced Segmentations.
- You can create custom reports based on almost all dimensions or metrics.
- You can create and track conversions (i.e. goals).
- You can track your ecommerce website's transactions.
- You can use default metrics or calculated metrics for your reports.
- You can set up alerts to automatically send you notice on spike traffic trends.

Data Collection

If your website happened to have started using Google Analytics since many years ago, then all your historical data from the beginning are still always available to you. This makes it easy for you to do year-over-year (YOY) data trend comparison.

Google Analytics is unable to roll back the data. i.e.

- If a few pages of your website have not been set up with Google Analytics tracking code, then you would not have data for those web pages, and you will have no way to get the missing data in retrospect.
- For the old years when your website has not been installed with Google Analytics tracking code, then you would not have those historical data, and you will have no way to get the historical data in retrospect.

Speed

Reports are updated very quickly, and are rarely or never delayed. Yesterday's data would always be fully available today. In many Google Analytics properties, reports are updated in which you can "feel" the data is almost up-to-date in real time.

The quick update of reports enables you to quickly spot data spikes or outliers. You can also pre-set "alerts" in your Google Analytics account. When any abnormal data is detected, you will automatically receive the alerts.

Real-time reports are available, which is a rare feature in most other web analytics tools. The real-time reports can actually show the number of users that are currently on your site at this very moment.

Data Accuracy

Data precision is low due to data sampling in Google Analytics.

Pre-aggregated data:

- The data in most of the standard reports is pre-aggregated by Google Analytics. The metrics and dimensions shown in the standard reports are already calculated before you request the reports for any date range.

- If your report contains more than 50,000 unique data rows daily, then your data is sampled. Often reports with large amount of unique page URLs or unique keywords show large amounts of unique rows and will easily exceed the 50,000 data row limit. When this happens, the report will group values into a single row labeled (other), and you lose accuracy for detailed data.

Non-aggregated data:

- If the date range contains more than 500,000 sessions, Google Analytics will apply sampling to calculate the metrics for your report.
- If you apply a second dimension to a standard report, apply a segment to a standard report, or create a custom report, the metrics for the report must be calculated on the fly. The data Google Analytics uses is non-aggregated data, and this is why sampled data comes up in your reports.

Data sampling is the main reason in which your reports are available very quickly. You have options to increase the data precision by having more data in sampling or decrease the data precision with less data in sampling.

- When data precision improves, it will take longer processing time for your reports.
- When data precision decreases, it will take less processing time to compile your reports.

The data limit for Google Analytics Premium version is much higher, and that allows you to download totally non-sampled reports.

Storage

The data is stored on Google's databases/servers. Reports are always available, but use of the data is limited.

You cannot take immediate actions based on the user behavior that was collected by your Google Analytics. Your Google Analytics data is store on Google's databases/servers, and even you can extract the data through Google's API, however it is difficult to connect your Google Analytics data back to the Ecommerce transaction data or the user behavior data that you have collected without Google Analytics.

Access

If you are based in China using any China IP addresses, accessing Google Analytics interface can often be a problem. Most of the times when logging in or accessing the reports, you can encounter either slow loading or unavailability.

However, if you are accessing Google Analytics with most any other countries' IP addresses, you should always be okay.

Previous Chapters

Next Chapters

Gordon Choi's Analytics Book has been available since August 2016 and is proudly powered by Folks Analytics.

Google Analytics Tracking Codes

Chapter 04

JS

To track websites' data, Google Analytics uses a JavaScript based tracking code. This tracking code must be inserted onto each web page that requires data tracking.

Create a New Google Analytics Account

First you will need a new Google Analytics account.

When you register a new email address on Gmail, you are automatically assigned with a new login to your Google Account. With this login, sign in to Google Analytics through:

```
http://www.google.com/analytics/
```

And your Google Analytics account will be created.

Account Structure

Google Analytics has a three-level structure:

- Accounts
- Properties
- Views

Under an account, you can have multiple properties.

Properties

In your Google Analytics account, each website should be set up under a new property.

Assume you have:

- www.example.com which is your website for desktop users (or desktop website).
- m.example.com which is your website for mobile users (or mobile website).

You have three options to set up your websites with Google Analytics. The most straightforward and easiest is to create two new properties and set up:

- www.example.com to the first new property.
- m.example.com to the second new property.

At this point, each property (or website) will get a unique Google Analytics property ID (e.g. UA-XXXXXXXX-2 and UA-XXXXXXXX-2).

Views

A property can contain multiple views. Once you have created your first new property, you should already have a new view under your property. By default, this first new view contains all the data for the property.

You can create multiple views in which the second view can contain only a subset of data of this property by applying data filters. For example, your second view can be restricted to only contain users who visited your website from mobile devices.

Account, Property & View

Let's look at a visual example of all the views and properties under your Google Analytics account:

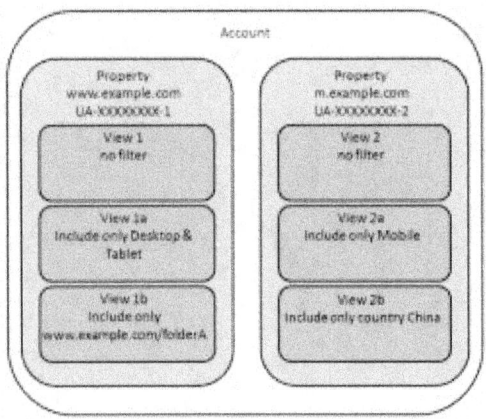

The unique Google Analytics IDs are on the property level. In this case, they are UA-XXXXXXXX-1 and UA-XXXXXXXX-2.

Access Rights

You can assign one of the four access rights type to Google Account users in order for them to access Google Analytics reports.

- Read & Analyze: The lowest level of access in which a user is able to view reports, and create custom reports, segments, or alerts.
- Collaborate: A user is allowed to share customization and do whatever the "Read & Analyze" can do.
- Edit.
- Manage Users.

If you only need a user to read the reports, then assign him with Read & Analyze. If you need a user to edit the Admin section, then assign him/her with the Edit access. If you need a user to add or delete other users' access rights, then assign him/her with Manage Users.

For each Google Analytics user, you can grant access at either the property level or the view level. For example, if a user is given Edit access right to property m.example.com (UA-XXXXXXXX-2), then he / she already has Edit access right to View 2, View 2a and View 2b.

Google Analytics Tracking Code Setup

You are required to get the JavaScript based tracking code (Google Analytics tracking code) from your Google Analytics property, and place this tracking code on to every pages of your website.

To get your Google Analytics tracking code, log on to your Google Analytics account, select your website under Property, and go to:

```
Admin -> Tracking Info -> Tracking Code
```

By default, your Google Analytics tracking code should look something like this. It is the latest version of Google Analytics tracking code and is called the Universal Analytics version. This default Universal Analytics tracking code logs a page view each time a page loads.

```
<script>(function(i,s,o,g,r,a,m){i['GoogleAnalyticsObject']=r;i[r]=i[r]
||function(){(i[r].q=i[r].q||[]).push(arguments)},i[r].l=1*new
Date();a=s.createElement(o),m=s.getElementsByTagName(o)[0];a.async=1;a.
src=g;m.parentNode.insertBefore(a,m)})(window,document,'script','//www.
google-analytics.com/analytics.js','ga');ga('create', 'UA-XXXXXXXX-Y',
'auto');ga('send', 'pageview');</script>
```

Let's look at only the first part of the tracking code. The main objective of the first part of this code is to fetch file analytics.js which contains the Google Analytics tracking library from Google's servers and inserts the library into your web page.

```
(function(i,s,o,g,r,a,m){i['GoogleAnalyticsObject']=r;i[r]=i[r]||functi
on(){(i[r].q=i[r].q||[]).push(arguments)},i[r].l=1*new
Date();a=s.createElement(o),m=s.getElementsByTagName(o)[0];a.async=1;a.
src=g;m.parentNode.insertBefore(a,m)})(window,document,'script','//www.
google-analytics.com/analytics.js','ga');
```

The analytics.js JavaScript library uses first-party cookies.

A cookie is a small text file that is stored in a user's web browser and has:

- A name-value pair containing the actual data.
- An expiry date after which the cookie is no longer valid.
- The domain and path of the server it should be sent to.

While on your website, a user navigates from page to page. Google Analytics uses cookies from the analytics.js JavaScript library to remember what the user has done from page to page.

The analytics.js file sets two cookies.

Cookie Name	Expiration Time	Objective
_ga	2 years	Distinguish users

Cookie Name	Expiration Time	Objective
_gat	10 minutes	Throttle request rate

The second part of the tracking code has two lines of commands which are the backbones of the Google Analytics tracking code. When a web pages (with Google Analytics tracking code installed) loads,

- The first line initiates a Google Analytics tracker that sends data to your property i.e. in this case the property ID is initiated in the format UA-XXXXXXXX-Y with the scope of Google Analytics cookies of your website defined.
- The second line sends a page view to Google Analytics.

```
ga('create', 'UA-XXXXXXXX-Y', 'auto');ga('send', 'pageview');
```

Note for the tracking code to properly work, the first command line ('create') must always be placed before the ('send') command line and any other additional command line. The simple reason is a tracker must always be initiated before anything else can happen.

The third parameter 'auto' in the first command line defines the scope of cookies. You are allowed to set other values to the third parameter for specific requirements.

Examples:

- If it is set to 'auto' and the tracking code is placed on all pages of domain example.com, then the cookies will cover both www.example.com and m.example.com.
- If it is left blank and the tracking code is placed on all pages of domain example.com, then the cookies will cover both www.example.com and m.example.com.
- If it is set to 'example.com' and the tracking code is placed on all pages of domain example.com, then the cookies will cover both www.example.com and m.example.com.
- If it is set to 'www.example.com' and the tracking code is placed on all pages of domain example.com, then the cookies will cover only www.example.com.
- If it is set to 'm.example.com' and the tracking code is placed on all pages of domain example.com, then the cookies will cover only m.example.com.

Where to Place the Tracking Code?

Google Analytics tracking code is asynchronous in which the browser does not have to wait for the entire code to completely load to continue rendering the rest of the web page.

- Google recommends placing the tracking code in the <head></head> section of your web pages in order to take the asynchronous advantage.
- It is okay to place the tracking code anywhere in the <body></body> section of your web pages.

- If your website was created by using one of the many open-source or paid content management systems (CMS), you will need to have edit access to your CMS in order to add / edit the Google Analytics tracking code.
- If your website was coded from scratch, then it may be more complicated and your web developer will have to add / edit the Google Analytics tracking code for you.

How to Setup the Tracking Code?

Assume you actually have two websites: One for desktop and tablet users (www.example.com) and the other for mobile users (m.example.com) in which both sites are under top level domain example.com. Consider the different setup options.

- The single property ID setup
- The two properties ID setup
- The advanced setup

The Single Property ID Setup

The setup:

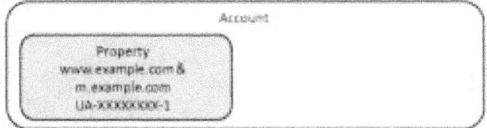

- Create one Google Analytics property with one property ID (e.g. UA-XXXXXXXX-1).
- Place the tracking code with property ID UA-XXXXXXXX-1 on to all pages of your websites (including both www.example.com and m.example.com).

The pros:

- It is very simple to manage one website under one property in which maintaining the correct tracking code with the correct property ID is straight forward.
- In your reports, you already have the counts of total sessions and total users per the two websites aggregated.

The cons:

- One property has to store two websites' data. If data size grows quickly, the property can quickly run into data sampling.
- Both sites' data are mixed in all the reports, and it will be very difficult to split the data when you require analyzing the data in details.

The Two Property IDs Setup

The setup:

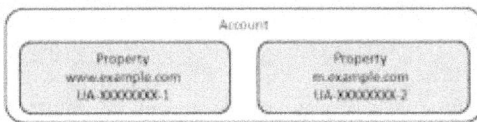

- Create your two websites where each is under a unique property IDs. For example, one ID for www.example.com (UA-XXXXXXXX-1) and another one ID for m.example.com (UA-XXXXXXXX-2).
- Place the tracking code of UA-XXXXXXXX-1 on to all pages of www.example.com and the tracking code of UA-XXXXXXXX-2 on to all pages of m.example.com.

The pros:

- The two property setup makes it much easier when separately analyzing each of the website's data.
- By using two property IDs, you have less risk to run into data sampling.

The cons:

- You will have to maintain two separate tracking codes with two different property IDs on your two websites.
- You cannot easily work out the counts of total sessions and total users per single website.

The Advanced Setup

The setup:

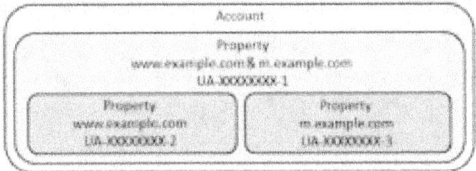

- Create one Google Analytics property with one property ID (e.g. UA-XXXXXXXX-1).
- Create two more properties each for one website. You should have one ID for www.example.com (UA-XXXXXXXX-2) and another one ID for m.example.com (UA-XXXXXXXX-3).
- Place the tracking code with property ID UA-XXXXXXXX-1 on to all pages of your websites (including both www.example.com and m.example.com).
- Place the tracking code of UA-XXXXXXXX-2 on to all pages of www.example.com and the tracking code of UA-XXXXXXXX-3 on to all pages of m.example.com.
- Then make the following changes to your tracking codes.

On all the pages of www.example.com:

```
ga('create', 'UA-XXXXXXXX-1', 'auto');ga('send', 'pageview');

ga('create', 'UA-XXXXXXXX-2', 'auto', 'wwwexample');ga('wwwexample.send',
'pageview');
```

On all the pages of m.example.com:

```
ga('create', 'UA-XXXXXXX-1', 'auto');ga('send', 'pageview');

ga('create', 'UA-XXXXXXX-3', 'auto', 'mexample');ga('mexample.send',
'pageview');
```

The additional lines simply mean:

- Initiate an additional Google Analytics tracker for wwwexample or mexample. You can use tracker names other than wwwexample or mexample.
- Send a page view to tracker wwwexample or mexample.

The pros:

- The setup enables very simple data aggregation and analysis. The count of total sessions and users per of the largest property with both websites (UA-XXXXXXX-1) have already been calculated for you. The same metrics for each of the properties (UA-XXXXXXX-2 and UA-XXXXXXX-2) as separate sets of data have also been calculated for you.
- Even when your largest property (UA-XXXXXXX-1) runs into data sampling, the other smaller properties (UA-XXXXXXX-2 and UA-XXXXXXX-3) will still have no problem with data sampling.

The cons:

- It is complicated to maintain the tracking codes, with two different property IDs per website and three unique property IDs on two websites.
- The largest property (UA-XXXXXXX-1) contains data of both the websites, and it is the property with the highest risk of running into data sampling.

The Legacy Tracking Codes

Prior to the asynchronous tracking codes, Google Analytics tracking code used to be synchronous, and this is the synchronous tracking code.

```
<script type="text/javascript">var gaJsHost = (("https:" ==
document.location.protocol) ? "https://ssl." :
"http://www.");document.write(unescape("%3Cscript src='" + gaJsHost +
"google-analytics.com/ga.js'
type='text/javascript'%3E%3C/script%3E"));</script><script
type="text/javascript">try{var pageTracker =
_gat._getTracker("UA-XXXXXXX-X");pageTracker._trackPageview();}
catch(err) {}</script>
```

There were used to be older versions of Google Analytics tracking codes. This one was the first version of asynchronous tracking code:

```
<script type="text/javascript">var _gaq = _gaq ||
[];_gaq.push(['_setAccount',
'UA-XXXXXXXX-X']);_gaq.push(['_trackPageview']);(function() {var ga =
document.createElement('script'); ga.type = 'text/javascript'; ga.async =
true;ga.src = ('https:' == document.location.protocol ? 'https://ssl' :
'http://www') + '.google-analytics.com/ga.js';var s =
document.getElementsByTagName('script')[0];
s.parentNode.insertBefore(ga, s);})();</script>
```

Both the older versions of tracking codes do the same thing as the latest version: Initiate the Google Analytics tracker, and send a page view to Google Analytics.

If you are still using one of the older versions of Google Analytics tracking codes, you should upgrade to the latest version (i.e. Universal Analytics) which is also the second version of asynchronous tracking code.

The Universal Analytics tracking code covers whatever the older codes do (i.e. initiates a tracker and sends a page view). On top of that:

- The Universal Analytics tracking code uses a single and unique cookie and is able to assign a visitor ID to the users' browsers.
- Universal Analytics has the ability to track users across multiple devices, such as using a user login which is a unique identifier on all devices that allows all the activities of a user to be tied together.

Previous Chapters

Gordon Choi's Analytics Book has been available since August 2016 and is proudly powered by Folks Analytics.

Google Analytics Traffic Sources

Chapter 05

One of the main jobs of Google Analytics is to get the traffic sources correct in your reports.

- Google Analytics determines where a user came from (i.e. referrer) when he / she arrives at your website.
- Google analytics gets the referrer information (i.e. the URL of the previous web page) from the user's browser.
- The two dimensions (i.e. Source and Medium) are assigned values of referrer information by Google Analytics.
- By default, Google Analytics categorizes traffic sources into organic search, referral and direct.

Organic search traffic

Organic search is the traffic that comes from search engines where source is the name of a search engine (that is in the default list of search engines of Google Analytics, or that has been manually added to your Google Analytics property's new search engine), and medium is "organic". For example:

```
source=baidumedium=organic
```

Referral traffic

Referral is the traffic that comes from a non search engine website. i.e. The domain name of this website is not in the default search engine list of Google Analytics, or it has never been manually added to your Google Analytics property as a new search engine. Source is the domain name of the non search engine website, and medium is "referral". For example:

```
source=zhihu.commedium=referral
```

Direct traffic

Direct is the traffic that has no source. It happens when a user types in your site's URL into the browser, uses a bookmark in the browser, or clicks a hyperlink (of your site's URL) that automatically opens a browser. Source is "direct" and medium = "(none)".

```
source=directmedium=(none)
```

The last-click attribution

In web analytics, attribution refers to the method of crediting traffic sources to metrics or actions. The metrics can be a session, a page view, a goal conversion or other measurable events.

Let's consider an example.

- A user could have visited your website multiple times through multiple sources.
- For all the sessions of this user that have happened on your site, Google Analytics recorded all the traffic sources.
- By default, Google Analytics uses the last-click attribution model to report traffic sources for this user.
- The exception is if this user's last-click to your site has recorded source "direct" and medium "(none)", then Google Analytics would report the source and medium information from the user's previous session to your site. This means by default direct traffic cannot overwrite the traffic source that is not direct traffic.

Previous Chapters

Next Chapters

Gordon Choi's Analytics Book has been available since August 2016 and is proudly powered by Folks Analytics.

Google Analytics Custom Dimensions and Custom Metrics

By default, Google Analytics makes built-in dimensions and metrics available. However, if some dimensions and metrics are not available, you can create custom dimensions and/or custom metrics. Once they are created, you can use them to collect and analyze data that Google Analytics does not automatically track.

Custom Dimensions

- The dimension index. Each custom dimension must be assigned with an index. The format is dimension[0-9]+. Examples are dimension1, dimension13, etc.
- Google Analytics has made up to 20 custom dimensions available per property. For Google Analytics Premium version, the limit is up to 200 custom dimensions.

Custom Metrics

- Each custom metric must be assigned with an index. The format is metric[0-9]+. Examples are metric1, metric13, etc.
- A metric is numerical which can be integer, currency or time.
- Google Analytics has made up to 20 custom metrics available per property. For Google Analytics Premium version, the limit is up to 200 custom metrics.

Steps to Create and Use Custom Dimensions and/or Custom Metrics

Below are the steps when using custom dimensions and custom metrics.

- Step 1 Configuration: Create and define your custom dimensions and/or custom metrics in your Google Analytics account. Admin access to your Google Analytics account is required.
- Step 2 Code implementation: Add the additional codes (for custom dimensions and/or custom metrics) to your current Google Analytics tracking code.
- Step 3 Data Collection: Allow your website to collect users' custom dimension and/or custom metric data.
- Step 4 Reporting: View reports that contain custom dimension and/or custom metric data.

Create a New Custom Dimension

```
Go to Admin -> Custom Definitions -> Custom Dimensions -> + New Custom
Dimension
```

Under Add Custom Dimension,

- Enter the dimension's name in the Name field.
- Select Scope from one of the options: Hit, Session, User, or Product.
- Check the Active radio button.
- Click Create. Now you have successfully created a new dimension.

Create a New Custom Metric

```
Go to Admin -> Custom Definitions -> Custom Metrics -> + New Custom Metric
```

Under Add Custom Metric,

- Enter the metric's name in the Name field.
- Select Scope from one of the options: Hit, or Product.
- Select Formatting Type from one of the options: Integer, Currency or Time.
- Check the Active radio button.
- Click Create. Now you have successfully created a new metric.

Scope of Hit for Custom Dimensions

A hit is a user's interaction with your mobile website that results in data being sent to Google Analytics. Examples of hits include:

- Page views
- Screen views
- Events
- Transactions

A user on your mobile website can send one or more hits, and value of a custom dimension is sent once per hit.

Scope of Session for Custom Dimensions

A session is a group of hits recorded for a user in a given time period. When a custom dimension is created with session scope, its value is applied to all the hits in a current session. A custom dimension's value is sent once per session during a user's session on your mobile website.

A session expires after 30 minutes of a user's inactivity on your mobile website or at midnight (i.e. 00h00). A session can also expire when a user returns to your mobile website through a different campaign.

Scope of User for Custom Dimensions

When a user visits your mobile website for the first time, Google Analytics sets a new cookie on his / her web browser. A session is created for each user's visit to your mobile website. For each user's session:

- A new user is counted in Google Analytics when the user visits your website for the first time. No Google Analytics cookie exists prior to this current session.
- A returning user is counted in Google Analytics when it is not the first time the user visits your website. A previous Google Analytics cookie already exists.

For a custom dimension with user scope, a user's lifetime on your mobile website can last or expire.

- The user's lifetime is applied to all the hits in the current session and all future sessions.
- A user's lifetime ends when he / she visits your mobile website through a different device or a different web browser. Google Analytics generates a new cookie for the user.
- A user's lifetime ends, when a user deletes cookies on his / her web browser.

A custom dimension's value is sent once per user during a user's lifetime on your mobile website.

Custom Dimension Example

Assume your mobile website is a hotel booking website which has different level of pages:

```
Homepage: http://www.example.com/Hotel search result page per city:
http://www.example.com/hotel-list/beijing/Hotel detail page:
http://www.example.com/hotel-detail/h00011
```

Assume the specific hotel detail page (with id h00011) is a hotel located in city Beijing.

```
http://www.example.com/hotel-detail/h00011
```

Assume the specific hotel detail page (with id h00012) is a hotel located in city Shanghai.

```
http://www.example.com/hotel-detail/h00012
```

Assume the specific hotel detail page (with id h00013) is a hotel located in city Shenzhen.

```
http://www.example.com/hotel-detail/h00013
```

In this case, you will need Google Analytics to report on sessions by Beijing hotels, sessions by Shanghai hotels, sessions by Shenzhen hotels, etc. Not a single standard Google Analytics report can provide such information.

Step 1: Configuration

You can set up a custom dimension to track sessions per city.

```
Go to Admin -> Custom Definitions -> Custom Dimensions -> + New Custom
Dimension
```

Under Add Custom Dimension,

- Enter "hotelcity" in the Name field for the dimension.
- Select Session as scope.
- Check the Active radio button.
- Click Create. Now you have successfully created a new dimension with session scope.

Step 2: Code Implementation

The next step is you will have to add an additional code to the Universal Analytics version of your standard Google Analytics tracking code. The format of the additional code is:

```
ga('set', 'dimension1', 'value');
```

On all the web pages which contain a Beijing hotel, assign 'hotel-beijing' as value.

```
ga('set', 'dimension1', 'hotel-beijing');
```

One the web page, the entire Google Analytics tracking code will become:

```
<script>(function(i,s,o,g,r,a,m){i['GoogleAnalyticsObject']=r;i[r]=i[r]
||function(){(i[r].q=i[r].q||[]).push(arguments)},i[r].l=1*new
Date();a=s.createElement(o),m=s.getElementsByTagName(o)[0];a.async=1;a.
src=g;m.parentNode.insertBefore(a,m)})(window,document,'script','//www.
google-analytics.com/analytics.js','ga');ga('create', 'UA-XXXXXXXX-Y',
'auto');ga('set', 'dimension1', 'hotel-beijing');ga('send',
'pageview');</script>
```

The sequence of each line of code is important. The line of code that sets the custom
dimension has to be defined before the page view is sent.

```
ga('create', 'UA-XXXXXXXX-Y', 'auto');ga('set', 'dimension1',
'hotel-beijing');ga('send', 'pageview');
```

For web pages with a Shanghai hotel, assign 'hotel-shanghai'.

```
ga('set', 'dimension1', 'hotel-shanghai');
```

For web pages with a Shenzhen hotel, assign 'hotel-shenzhen'.

```
ga('set', 'dimension1', 'hotel-shenzhen');
```

On all other web pages that do not require tracking sessions by hotel city, you will still use
the standard tracking code without changes.

```
<script>(function(i,s,o,g,r,a,m){i['GoogleAnalyticsObject']=r;i[r]=i[r]
||function(){(i[r].q=i[r].q||[]).push(arguments)},i[r].l=1*new
Date();a=s.createElement(o),m=s.getElementsByTagName(o)[0];a.async=1;a.
src=g;m.parentNode.insertBefore(a,m)})(window,document,'script','//www.
google-analytics.com/analytics.js','ga');ga('create', 'UA-XXXXXXXX-Y',
'auto');ga('send', 'pageview');</script>
```

Steps 3 & 4: Data Collection and Reporting

Assume you have allowed time for Google Analytics to collect data into your newly
implemented custom dimension.

From any Google Analytics report that has Second Dimension available for selection, click to expand the Second Dimension drop-down. Your newly created "hotelcity" custom dimension should appear under Custom Dimensions.

Now you can use your custom dimensions in your Google Analytics reports. Example:

- Under the Source/Medium report, select "hotelcity" from the Second Dimension drop-down.
- Now you should see "hotel-beijing", "hotel-shanghai" and "hotel-shenzhen" appear under the Second Dimension column alongside all the source/medium values in the Source/Medium report.

Gordon Choi's Analytics Book has been available since August 2016 and is proudly powered by Folks Analytics.

Google Analytics Goal Tracking

Chapter 07

A typical ecommerce website needs to track purchases or registrations as conversions. Such conversions can be defined in Google Analytics as goals (or goal conversions).

Setting up goals to track either purchases or registrations is similar in Google Analytics. Let's consider a case to set up goal conversions to track purchases on your site.

Types of Goal Conversions

Google Analytics has four goal types available.

- Destination goals: They are specific URLs' page views that were predefined as goals. For example, when a user completes a transaction on your site, he / she is then taken to a purchase completion page. When Google Analytics records a page view that happens on this purchase completion page's URL, a goal conversion is also recorded.
- Event goals: They are events that are triggered by non page view interactions on your site.
- Pages per session goals: For example, a goal conversion is recorded if a user has viewed more than 3 pages on your site.
- Session duration goals: For example, a goal conversion is recorded if a user has spent more than 10 minutes on your site.

Create a Destination Goal

Under your Google Analytics properties, go to:

```
View -> Goals -> +New Goal
```

- Enter a goal name in Name field.
- Choose a Goal Slot ID that is available.
- Select Destination as Type.
- Click Continue.
- Enter a web page URL. If your goal conversion is purchase completion, then enter the purchase completion page's URL.

Google Analytics requires one of the three ways to match your goal destination URL.

Equals to:

- The URL has to match exactly what is entered, and should only include the path but not the hostname.
- Enter /booking-completed/thank-you.html to exactly match /booking-completed/thank-you.html

Begins with:

- The URL must begin with the string entered. It can continue with additional text at the end of the URL and should only include the path but not the hostname.
- Enter /booking-completed/thank-you.html to match /booking-completed/thank-you.html?orderid=12345

Regular expression:

- The URL has to match the regular expression pattern, and should only include the path but not the hostname.
- Enter \/thankyou\.(html|aspx) to match /thankyou.html or /thankyou.aspx

Then you are given options to:

- Assign a numerical value for a conversion e.g. RMB 100 for a conversion.
- Add the steps as URLs (and with a Name to each URL) for your goal funnel.

Goal funnel

If you have your goal and goal funnel steps created correctly, then later you will expect to see the visual data in your goal funnel report.

- Goal funnel provides a good way for you to visually see exactly which step most of your users departed without completing the funnel in full.
- You can then use this information to make decisions on the exact spot on your site that you will have to focus fixing.

Now you can save your goal.

- The total number of goal conversions is 1,205 (i.e. Reservation Booked) which means the number of times users have reached this pre-defined goal URL.
- Users have entered the Booking Process step 2,858 times, and for 1,834 times they have left without completing the funnel in full. Only 1,024 (36%) times they have continued to the final step (i.e. the goal URL).
- Users have entered the Checking Availability step 10,076 times, and for 7,218 times they have left without completing the funnel in full. Only 2,858 (28%) times they have continued to the next step (i.e. the Booking process).

Once you have created a goal, the goal starts reporting goal data in your Google Analytics view going forward. Your Google Analytics view does not retroactively reprocess goal data that could have happened prior to the goal creation.

Track User Registration via Goal Conversion

Assume your Chinese mobile website allows users to sign up (or register).

Your website has a registration form on this web page.

```
URL A: http://www.example.com/register
```

When a user successfully registered, he /she will be shown this registration success page.

```
URL B: http://www.example.com/register?success
```

To create this goal, under to your Google Analytics properties go to:

```
View -> Goals -> +New Goal
```

- Enter "RegistrationSuccess" in Name field.
- Choose a Goal Slot ID that is available.
- Select Destination as Type and click Continue.
- Enter \/register\?success. This is in the regular expression format which matches URL B.

Previous Chapters

Gordon Choi's Analytics Book has been available since August 2016 and is proudly powered by *Folks Analytics*.

Google Analytics Enhanced Ecommerce Tracking

Chapter 08

A typical ecommerce website needs to track online purchases (i.e. transactions). Google Analytics provides two major features for ecommerce websites to track transactions.

- Ecommerce Tracking
- Enhanced Ecommerce Tracking

I highly recommend any ecommerce website to set up Google Analytics ecommerce tracking (or enhanced ecommerce tracking) and record transaction data.

- With ecommerce tracking (or enhanced ecommerce tracking), you can record the information about all the transactions that happen on your site including order IDs, transaction values, product IDs, product quantity, and many more.
- With the transaction data recorded by Google Analytics, they can be connected other existing Google analytics metrics and dimensions for more advanced reporting and analysis.

The Scope of Ecommerce Tracking

Without Ecommerce Tracking, your Google Analytics data and your transaction data are separated.

- On your website's server, all transactions are processed. All transaction data is recorded and stored in your database.
- All users' behavior data is sent to and stored in Google's servers. Only behavior data shows up in Google Analytics reports.
- No connection is established between Google Analytics data and your transaction data.
- The disconnected data does not allow any further sophisticated analysis.

Once Ecommerce Tracking is implemented, a connection can be established between your Google Analytics data and your transaction data.

- On your website's server, all transactions are processed. All transaction data is recorded and stored in your database.
- All users' behavior data is sent to and stored in Google's servers.
- A connection is established between Google Analytics data and your transaction data through your customers' order IDs.
- Both behavior data and transaction data appear in your Google Analytics reports.
- The connected data can be used for further complicated analysis.

Ecommerce Tracking Implementation

Below are the steps to implement Ecommerce Tracking onto your mobile website.

- Enable Ecommerce Tracking
- Initiate Ecommerce Tracking
- Add a transaction
- Add items for the Transaction
- Send data
- Remove data
- Verify Data

Enable Ecommerce Tracking

Under your Google Analytics property, go to:

```
View -> Ecommerce Settings
```

- Select On under Enable Ecommerce. This will enable your Google Analytics view to use the ecommerce tracking.

Ecommerce tracking allows you to send the transaction information of your users and have your users' transactions and other information related to their transactions available in Google Analytics reports.

- Besides the basic Google Analytics tracking code, you are required to use an additional JavaScript code (i.e. Ecommerce tracking code) to send the transaction data to Google Analytics.
- The Ecommerce tracking code should only be triggered and send transaction data on the web page once a transaction is complete.
- The Ecommerce tracking code allows you to send compulsory data and optional data.

Initiate Ecommerce Tracking

To initiate Google Analytics Ecommerce Tracking on a web page, use the line of code below. Usually you should place this line of code on the page immediate after a transaction completes. This line creates a shopping cart object which awaits you to add transaction and item data into it.

```
ga('require', 'ecommerce');
```

The above line of code for Ecommerce Tracking initiation is the first line of Ecommerce Tracking code, and must be placed before all other Ecommerce Tracking related lines of code. It must be placed after the line of code in which Google Analytics tracker is initiated.

The order must be:

```
ga('create', 'UA-XXXXXXXX-Y', 'auto');Some Google Analytics
codesga('require', 'ecommerce');Rest of the Ecommerce Tracking
```

Add a Transaction

The data fields per transaction:

id

- It holds an identifier as a string for each unique transaction that happens on your site.
- It is a compulsory field.

revenue

- It represents the total revenue as a numerical value for a specific transaction.
- It is a compulsory field.

affiliation

- It can be used for a particular affiliate code or referral (as a string) for a particular transaction.
- It is an optional field.

tax

- It represents the tax charges as a numerical value for a specific transaction.
- It is an optional field.

shipping

- It represents the shipping charges as a numerical value for a specific transaction.
- It is an optional field.

currency

- It allows you to specify a currency for your transaction.
- It is an optional field. Normally, you will only use this field when the currency you have selected under your Google Analytics view is different to this new currency.

Add Items for the Transaction

The data fields per product per transaction:

sku

- It holds a unique identifier of a particular product.
- It is a compulsory field.

name

- It holds the name of a particular product.
- It is a compulsory field.

price

- It holds the unit price of a particular product as a numerical value.
- It is a compulsory field.

quantity

- It represents the number of units (as an integer) of a particular product purchased through a particular transaction.

- It is a compulsory field.

category

- It represents the category where a particular product belongs.
- It is an optional field.

currency

- It allows you to specify a currency for your transaction.
- It is an optional field. Normally, you will only use this field when the currency you have selected under your Google Analytics view is different to this new currency.
- The list of currency codes for all the supported currencies: External Link.

Send Data

The next step is you send the entire set of transaction data to Google Analytics with the line of code below:

```
ga('ecommerce:send');
```

Verify Data

Once you have implemented all lines of codes that are required for Ecommerce Tracking, the next step is to verify if the transaction data has been correctly recorded by Google Analytics.

It really depends on how frequency a transaction happens on your mobile website, but normally within the next hour or the next several hours your Ecommerce Tracking data should appear in your Google Analytics reports.

Ecommerce Tracking Example

The example Ecommerce tracking code sends the transaction data with two products to Google Analytics.

```
ga('require', 'ecommerce');ga('ecommerce:addTransaction', {'id':
't0000399168', 'affiliation': 'None','revenue': '270.00','shipping':
'5.00','tax': '27.00','currency': 'CNY'});ga('ecommerce:addItem', {'id':
' t0000399168','name': 'Big Chocolate Bar','sku': 'gt345','category':
'Snack','price': '70.00','quantity': '1''currency':
'CNY'});ga('ecommerce:addItem', {'id': ' t0000399168','name': 'Wine
1982','sku': 'gt017','category': 'Alcohol','price': '100.00','quantity':
'2''currency': 'CNY'});ga('ecommerce:send');
```

The entire tracking code with the Google Analytics tracker and Ecommerce Tracking will become:

```
<script>(function(i,s,o,g,r,a,m){i['GoogleAnalyticsObject']=r;i[r]=i[r]
||function(){(i[r].q=i[r].q||[]).push(arguments)},i[r].l=1*new
Date();a=s.createElement(o),m=s.getElementsByTagName(o)[0];a.async=1;a.
src=g;m.parentNode.insertBefore(a,m)})(window,document,'script','//www.
google-analytics.com/analytics.js','ga');ga('create', 'UA-XXXXXXX-Y',
'auto');ga('send', 'pageview');ga('require',
'ecommerce');ga('ecommerce:addTransaction', {'id': 't0000399168',
'affiliation': 'None','revenue': '270.00','shipping': '5.00','tax':
'27.00','currency': 'CNY'});ga('ecommerce:addItem', {'id': '
t0000399168','name': 'Big Chocolate Bar','sku': 'gt345','category':
'Snack','price': '70.00','quantity': '1''currency':
'CNY'});ga('ecommerce:addItem', {'id': ' t0000399168','name': 'Wine
1982','sku': 'gt017','category': 'Alcohol','price': '100.00','quantity':
'2''currency': 'CNY'});ga('ecommerce:send');</script>
```

The Scope of Enhanced Ecommerce Tracking

Enhanced Ecommerce Tracking is an upgraded version of Ecommerce Tracking.

The advantages of Enhanced Ecommerce Tracking include tracking additional data besides the most common information, the completed transactions. In an ecommerce website's conversion funnel (for transactions), the web pages may be in this order:

- List page - A user browses a specific list page (of products).
- Product details page - A user browses a specific product's details page.
- Shopping cart - A user adds a product to the shopping cart.
- Checkout page - A user enters the checkout page.
- Purchase completed - A user completes the entire transaction.

With Enhanced Ecommerce Tracking, you can track data regarding list pages, product details pages, shopping cart, checkout page, and more.

Enable Ecommerce Tracking

To enable Enhanced Ecommerce Tracking, Google Analytics must have Ecommerce Tracking also enabled.

Under your Google Analytics property, go to:

```
View -> Ecommerce Settings
```

Select On under Enable Ecommerce. This will enable your Google Analytics view to use the Ecommerce Tracking.

Now go to (which is still under the same screen):

```
View -> Enhanced Ecommerce Settings
```

Select On under "Enable Enhanced Ecommerce Reporting", and click "Submit". This will enable your Google Analytics view to use Enhanced Ecommerce Tracking.

Initiate Ecommerce Tracking

If you already have ecommerce tracking implemented on your website, you can convert the ecommerce tracking implementation to enhanced ecommerce tracking. First in your tracking code, replace:

```
ga('require', 'ecommerce');
```

with:

```
ga('require', 'ec');
```

Enhanced Ecommerce Tracking Implementation for Transactions

The example Enhanced Ecommerce tracking code sends the transaction data with two products to Google Analytics.

```
<script>(function(i,s,o,g,r,a,m){i['GoogleAnalyticsObject']=r;i[r]=i[r]
||function(){(i[r].q=i[r].q||[]).push(arguments)},i[r].l=1*new
Date();a=s.createElement(o),m=s.getElementsByTagName(o)[0];a.async=1;a.
src=g;m.parentNode.insertBefore(a,m)})(window,document,'script','//www.
google-analytics.com/analytics.js','ga');ga('create', 'UA-XXXXXXXX-Y',
'auto');ga('require', 'ec');ga('set', '&cu', 'CNY'); //Specify
currencyga('ec:addProduct',{ //Add a product'id': 'gt345',  // Product
SKU'name': 'Big Chocolate Bar','category': 'Snack','brand':
'Whitelabel','variant': 'none','price': '70.00','quantity':
```

```
'1',});ga('ec:addProduct',{ //Add a product'id': 'gt017', // Product
SKU'name': 'Wine 1982','category': 'Alcohol','brand': 'French Red
Wine','variant': 'red wine','price': '100.00','quantity':
'2',});ga('ec:setAction', 'purchase',{ //Add the transaction'id':
't0000399168', // Transaction id'affiliation': 'none','revenue':
'270.00','tax': '27.00','shipping': '5.00','coupon': 'none',});ga('send',
'pageview');</script>
```

The currency of the transaction is specified by:

```
ga('set', '&cu', 'CNY');
```

The method that adds an item to the transaction:

```
ga('ec:addProduct',{// Some Codes});
```

The method that adds the transaction:

```
ga('ec:setAction', 'purchase',{// Some Codes});
```

Note, this line of code has been intentionally placed at the end of the entire tracking code.
This ensures all the information of this transaction have been specified before the data is
sent to Google Analytics.

```
ga('send', 'pageview');
```

Enhanced Ecommerce Tracking Implementation for Product Details View

To track user's view of a specific product details page, add the following code to all
product details pages.

```
<script>(function(i,s,o,g,r,a,m){i['GoogleAnalyticsObject']=r;i[r]=i[r]
||function(){(i[r].q=i[r].q||[]).push(arguments)},i[r].l=1*new
Date();a=s.createElement(o),m=s.getElementsByTagName(o)[0];a.async=1;a.
src=g;m.parentNode.insertBefore(a,m)})(window,document,'script','//www.
google-analytics.com/analytics.js','ga');ga('create', 'UA-XXXXXXX-Y',
'auto');ga('require', 'ec');ga('set', '&cu', 'CNY'); //Specify
```

```
currencyga('ec:addProduct',{'id': 'gt345',  // Product SKU'name': 'Big
Chocolate Bar','category': 'Snack','brand': 'Whitelabel','variant':
'none','price': '70.00','quantity': '1',});ga('ec:setAction', 'detail');
//Set the action to "details page"ga('send', 'pageview');</script>
```

Enhanced Ecommerce Tracking Implementation for Shopping Cart

A shopping cart of an ecommerce website allows a user to:

- Add an item (to the cart) when the user intents to buy that particular item.
- Remove an item (from the cart) when the user no longer wants to buy that particular item.

Adding an Item to the Shopping Cart

```
<script>(function(i,s,o,g,r,a,m){i['GoogleAnalyticsObject']=r;i[r]=i[r]
||function(){(i[r].q=i[r].q||[]).push(arguments)},i[r].l=1*new
Date();a=s.createElement(o),m=s.getElementsByTagName(o)[0];a.async=1;a.
src=g;m.parentNode.insertBefore(a,m)})(window,document,'script','//www.
google-analytics.com/analytics.js','ga');ga('create', 'UA-XXXXXXXX-Y',
'auto');ga('require', 'ec');ga('set', '&cu', 'CNY'); //Specify
currencyfunction addToCart(product) {  ga('ec:addProduct',{  'id':
'gt345',  // Product SKU  'name': 'Big Chocolate Bar',  'category':
'Snack',  'brand': 'Whitelabel',  'variant': 'none',  'price': '70.00',
'quantity': '1',  });  ga('ec:setAction', 'add'); // Set action to "add to
cart"  ga('send', 'event', 'enhanced ecommerce', 'button click', 'add to
Cart'); // Send "add to cart" with an event.}ga('send',
'pageview');</script>
```

Removing an Item from the Shopping Cart

```
<script>(function(i,s,o,g,r,a,m){i['GoogleAnalyticsObject']=r;i[r]=i[r]
||function(){(i[r].q=i[r].q||[]).push(arguments)},i[r].l=1*new
Date();a=s.createElement(o),m=s.getElementsByTagName(o)[0];a.async=1;a.
src=g;m.parentNode.insertBefore(a,m)})(window,document,'script','//www.
google-analytics.com/analytics.js','ga');ga('create', 'UA-XXXXXXXX-Y',
'auto');ga('require', 'ec');ga('set', '&cu', 'CNY'); //Specify
currencyfunction removeFromCart(product) {  ga('ec:addProduct',{  'id':
'gt345',  // Product SKU  'name': 'Big Chocolate Bar',  'category':
'Snack',  'brand': 'Whitelabel',  'variant': 'none',  'price': '70.00',
'quantity': '1',  });  ga('ec:setAction', 'remove'); // Set action to
"remove from cart"  ga('send', 'event', 'enhanced ecommerce', 'button
```

```
click', 'remove from Cart'); // Send "remove from cart" with an
event.}ga('send', 'pageview');</script>
```

Enhanced Ecommerce Tracking Implementation for Checkout

In the Checkout process of your ecommerce website, you will require users to submit a form with their personal information. Once the information is submitted to you, the transaction is considered "complete". The checkout process may vary on different ecommerce websites.

- Your Checkout process may have a form on only a single page.
- Your Checkout process may have a form that spans over multiple pages.

In this example, it demonstrates the implementation of Enhanced Ecommerce Tracking for the first page in the Checkout process.

```
<script>(function(i,s,o,g,r,a,m){i['GoogleAnalyticsObject']=r;i[r]=i[r]
||function(){(i[r].q=i[r].q||[]).push(arguments)},i[r].l=1*new
Date();a=s.createElement(o),m=s.getElementsByTagName(o)[0];a.async=1;a.
src=g;m.parentNode.insertBefore(a,m)})(window,document,'script','//www.
google-analytics.com/analytics.js','ga');ga('create', 'UA-XXXXXXXX-Y',
'auto');ga('require', 'ec');ga('set', '&cu', 'CNY'); //Specify
currencyfunction checkout(cart) {  for(var i = 0; i < cart.length; i++)
{    var product = cart[i];    ga('ec:addProduct',{    'id': 'gt345',  //
Product SKU    'name': 'Big Chocolate Bar',    'category': 'Snack',
'brand': 'Whitelabel',    'variant': 'none',    'price': '70.00',
'quantity': '1',    }); }  ga('ec:setAction','checkout', {'step': 1}); //
Set the action to "Checkout" and set value to 1 for the Checkout process's
first page.}ga('send', 'pageview');</script>
```

Add an onclick function to the Checkout button.

```
<button onclick="checkout(cart);">Checkout</button>
```

Previous Chapters

- Chapter 07 -

Next Chapters

<u>Gordon Choi's Analytics Book</u> has been available since August 2016 and is proudly powered by <u>Folks Analytics</u>.

Google Analytics Calculated Metrics

Chapter 09

Create a New Calculated Metrics

To create a new calculated metric, go to Admin and select your Google Analytics Properties.

```
View -> Calculated Metrics -> +New Calculated Metric
```

Under the Add Calculated Metric screen:

- Enter a new calculated metric name into the Name field.
- Enter an External Name which always has a calcMetric_ prefix. An External Name may only contain alphanumeric and underscore characters.
- Select a Formatting Type from one of the options: Float, Integer, Currency, Time, or Percent.
- Enter a Formula for your calculated metric. When you start typing in this Formula field, a list of predefined metrics may show up which can be used to create your formula. Accepted operators for your formulas include plus (+), minus (-), multiplied by (*), and divided by (/). A formula is limited to a maximum of 1024 characters.

Calculated Formula Example: Revenue per User

- Name: Revenue per User
- External Name: calcMetric_RPU
- Formatting Type: Currency

- Formula: {{Revenue}} / {{Users}}

Calculated Formula Example: Profit per User

Assume your mobile website's profit margin is 30%.

- Name: Profit per User
- External Name: calcMetric_PPU
- Formatting Type: Currency
- Formula: {{Profit}} / {{Users}} * 0.3

Calculated Formula Example: Transactions per User

- Name: Transactions per User
- External Name: calcMetric_TransPU
- Formatting Type: Float
- Formula: {{Transactions}} / {{Users}}

Calculated Formula Example: User-based Ecommerce Conversion Rate

- Name: User Ecom CR
- External Name: calcMetric_EcomCRPU
- Formatting Type: Percent
- Formula: {{Transactions}} / {{Users}}

Calculated Formula Example: User-based Goal Conversion Rate

- Name: User Goal CR
- External Name: calcMetric_GoalCRPU
- Formatting Type: Percent
- Formula: {{Goal Completions}} / {{Users}}

Calculated Formula Example: User-based Goal Conversion Rate (for a specific goal)

Assume in your Google Analytics profile you have created multiple Goals and one of your Goals is named Registration.

- Name: User Goal Reg CR
- External Name: calcMetric_GoalRegCRPU

- Formatting Type: Percent
- Formula: {{Registration (Goal 1 Completions)}} / {{Users}}

Calculated Formula Example: Search per User

- Name: Searches per User
- External Name: calcMetric_SearchesPU
- Formatting Type: Float
- Formula: {{Total Unique Searches}} / {{Users}}

Calculated Formula Example: Sessions with Search per User

- Name: Sessions Search per User
- External Name: calcMetric_SessSearchPU
- Formatting Type: Float
- Formula: {{Sessions with Search}} / {{Users}}

Calculated Formula Example: Average User Duration

- Name: Sessions Avg User Duration
- External Name: calcMetric_AvgUD
- Formatting Type: Time
- Formula: {{Session Duration }} / {{Users}}

To use your newly created custom dimensions and/or custom metrics, create a new Custom Report and select the custom dimensions and/or custom metrics.

Previous Chapters

- Chapter 08 - Google Analytics Enhanced Ecommerce Tracking

Next Chapters

- Chapter 10 - Google Analytics Campaign Tracking
- Chapter 11 - Track New Search Engines through Google Analytics
- Chapter 12 - Google Analytics Custom Reports

Gordon Choi's Analytics Book has been available since August 2016 and is proudly powered by *Folks Analytics*.

Google Analytics Campaign Tracking

Chapter 10

If you are placing paid search (a.k.a. PPC / pay per click) ads on Google AdWords, you should link your Google Analytics account to your AdWords account, and you should make sure Adwords auto-tagging is enabled. Then campaign tracking of your AdWords account is already enabled, and you won't have to explicitly deal with tagging your ad (or keyword) URLs.

Manual Campaign Tagging

But if you are placing ads elsewhere, such as on Baidu PPC, then you will have to manually tag all your URLs.

If not, then all Baidu paid search sessions and conversions will be reported as organic search sessions and conversions in your Google Analytics reports. When the paid search data is mixed up with the organic data, then you will almost have no chance to break them apart.

Campaign Tagging with UTM Parameters

Google Analytics has five built-in parameters for campaign URL tagging:

```
utm_source (compulsory)utm_medium (compulsory)utm_campaign
(compulsory)utm_term (optional)utm_content (optional)
```

How Google Analytics URL tagging should be implemented for Baidu paid search:

```
utm_source=baiduutm_medium=cpcutm_campaign=brand_exactutm_term=雷格斯
```

The whole URL becomes:

```
http://www.example.com/?utm_source=baidu&utm_medium=cpc&utm_campaign=br
and_exact&utm_term=雷格斯
```

Character Encoding Tool

Some specific browsers or some user's browser settings may not be able to encode your keyword data correctly before the keywords show up in your Google Analytics reports. For some reasons if you start seeing keywords show up in your Google Analytics reports as unrecognized or funny characters, then you can use a local character encoder / decoder tool to encode your Chinese keyword and then tag the encoded keyword onto your URL.

```
http://tool.chinaz.com/Tools/URLEncode.aspx
```

The encoded keyword:

```
utm_term=%e9%9b%b7%e6%a0%bc%e6%96%af
```

The whole URL becomes:

```
http://www.example.com/?utm_source=baidu&utm_medium=cpc&utm_campaign=br
and_exact&utm_term=%e9%9b%b7%e6%a0%bc%e6%96%af
```

Similar method (for URL tagging implementation) can be applied to other Chinese search engines.

Google's URL Builder Tool

Google has a URL Builder tool available which allows you to easily generate a campaign tagged URL:

```
https://support.google.com/analytics/answer/1033867?hl=en
```

Once you have correctly tagged all your paid search URLs, all future paid search sessions will be reported as paid search sessions.

However, for all the previous paid search sessions which were incorrectly reported as organic search sessions, Google Analytics does not provide a method to correct the traffic source in retrospect.

Previous Chapters

Next Chapters

Gordon Choi's Analytics Book has been available since August 2016 and is proudly powered by Folks Analytics.

Track New Search Engines through Google Analytics

Chapter 11

Google Analytics has a default list of search engines. When a user comes from one of the search engines in the list, the user's session and all the metrics associated to this user will be accredited to the correct search engine.

However, if a user comes through a website (such as sm.cn, a local Chinese mobile search engine) that has not yet been added to the default list, then in Google Analytics reports the session will be accredited to medium "referral".

Add a New Search Engine to Google Analytics

For the local search engines or new search engines that do not yet show up under organic search, you can manually configure Google Analytics to recognize them as search engines.

In Google Analytics, go to:

```
Admin -> Tracking Info -> Organic Search Sources -> Add Search Engine
```

Fill in the required fields (i.e. The search engine's domain name & query parameter), click Create, and the new search engine will be added.

Google Analytics assigns any organic search engine session to a single source so the order of the search engines placed under Domain Name is sometimes important. Any organic search session is assigned to the first search engine on your list that matches the Domain Name and Query Parameter.

Let's consider an example.

- If baidu.com is the first item on your list and image.baidu.com is second with both search engines using the same Query Parameter, such as word, all searches that happen on image.baidu.com are assigned to baidu.com.
- You can change the order of the search engines in the list to prioritize how sessions are assigned. If you place image.baidu.com first and baidu.com second, then all searches that happen on image.baidu.com will be assigned to image.baidu.com.

Previous Chapters

Next Chapters

Gordon Choi's Analytics Book has been available since August 2016 and is proudly powered by Folks Analytics.

Google Analytics Custom Reports

Chapter 12

In Google Analytics, you have access to many standard and pre-built reports. But often you will need reports that haven't been built. One option is creating your own Custom Reports.

Under your Google Analytics property, go to:

```
View -> Customization -> +New Custom Report
```

- Enter a report name in the Name field.
- Choose Flat Table as Type.

For Metric Groups, select from +add metric:

- Sessions
- Page Views
- % New Sessions
- Bounce Rate
- Transactions
- Any Goal you have previous set up and are also important to be included in regular reports.

For Dimension drill-downs, select from +add dimension:

- Date
- Landing Page

Assume you want to a custom report containing only organic search data. To filter / restrict the report to show only organic search data.

```
medium = organic
```

To filter restrict the report to show only organic search data from Baidu.

```
medium = organicsource = baidu
```

Alternatively, combine the dimensions into one.

```
source/medium = baidu / organic
```

Custom Report Example

A typical Custom Report that is created through this method may have rows and columns like the format below.

Date	Landing Page	Sessions	Page Views	% New Sessions	Bounce Rate	Transactions
April 1, 2016	/index.php	500	2533	37%	62%	7
April 2, 2016	/fruits/	123	870	31%	59%	2
April 3, 2016	/candies/	68	293	42%	57%	0

Previous Chapters

- Chapter 11 - Track New Search Engines through Google Analytics

Next Chapters

- Chapter 13 - Google Analytics Self Referrals
- Chapter 14 - Google Analytics Sampled Data
- Chapter 15 - Google Mobile App Analytics

Gordon Choi's Analytics Book has been available since August 2016 and is proudly powered by *Folks Analytics*.

Google Analytics Self Referrals

Chapter 13

Self Referrals are an issue, and self referrals can usually be caused by one of the scenarios.

- Client-side Redirects
- Untagged Web Pages

Client-side Redirect vs. Server-side Redirect

Consider the case below.

- You used to have an old URL m.example.com/page-A and you have been sending your users to this page.
- Then you have created a new page (m.example.com/page-B) to replace the Page-A. Now you are sending your users to page-B.
- However, there are many users who still are visiting your old page, Page-A.

To resolve this issue, you have set up URL direction from Page-A to Page-B. When your users visit Page-A, they will automatically be taken to Page-B. You can set up this redirect with a few methods.

URL Direction	Analytics
Server-side 301	Okay. http referrer header is preserved.
Server-side 302	Okay. http referrer header is preserved.
Client-side Redirect	Problem. http referrer header is not preserved.

You can always use the Chrome browser's built-in Developer Tool to verify if a redirect has been set up on the server-side as a 301 (or 302) redirect.

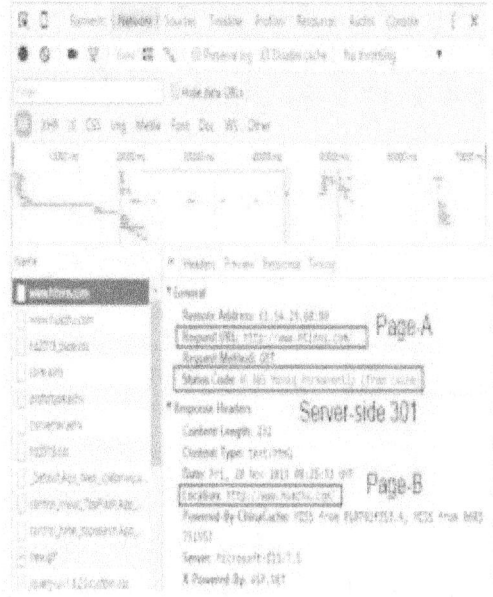

This line confirms it is a server-side redirect.

```
Status Code 301 Moved Permanently (from cache)
```

If you do not see the status code being reported as 301 or 302, then it is a client-side redirect.

- A client-side redirect happens with the browser itself.
- During a client-side redirect, Page-A and Page-B are loaded in succession, i.e. Page-A is loaded, and then it is followed by Page-B.
- This triggers two page views in succession without any click or interaction by a user, where the first page view (from Page-A) is never recorded by Google Analytics, and the source referrer (i.e. the previous page's URL) is lost.
- Your Google Analytics will end up reporting your own domain name (i.e. self-referral) as a source which is incorrect.

On Page-A, you have this code in the <head></head> section that performs a client-side redirect in the web browser.

```
<head>    <title>Page-A</title>    <meta http-equiv="refresh"
content="0;URL='http://m.example.com/Page-B'" />    </head>
```

- The meta element has the value of the http-equiv attribute set to "refresh" and the value of the content attribute set to "0" (meaning zero seconds), followed by the destination URL (i.e. the redirected URL) in which the browser is to request.
- The refresh time is set to zero seconds. Page-A is never displayed to the users before it is redirected to Page-B, which happened all on the client-side.

In practical when taking your users automatically from an old page to a new page, you should always only use server-side 301 (or 302) redirect. Server-side 301 (or 302) redirect preserves the referrer information which is good practice for web analytics.

Untagged Web Pages

Consider this scenario in which you have two pages on your website.

```
m.example.com/Page-Am.example.com/Page-B
```

- Page-A has no Google Analytics tracking code installed.
- Page-B has Google Analytics tracking code properly installed.

A user lands on Page-A. While on page-A, this user clicks a link that takes him / her to Page-B.

- On Page-A, no Google Analytics tracking code has been triggered, and nothing is recorded by Google Analytics.
- On Page-B, Google Analytics starts a new session for the user, and assigns your own domain name to the source referrer.

```
source=m.example.commedium=referral
```

This source referrer information recorded by Google Analytics is incorrect.

For good practice, you should always ensure installing your Google Analytics tracking code on all your web pages.

Gordon Choi's Analytics Book has been available since August 2016 and is proudly powered by Folks Analytics.

Google Analytics Sampled Data

Chapter 14

Data sampling can be a major issue. Google Analytics shows sampled data in the reports when appropriate criteria are met.

If a Google Analytics property is collecting an amount of data which has exceeded a single property's data size limit, then this Google Analytics property starts showing sampled data in the reports.

How does data sampling happen?

Data sampling happens when:

- More than 50,000 unique rows daily from pre-aggregated data show up in one of your reports.
- More than 500,000 sessions from non-aggregated data are used to compile a report. When data sampling happens, your reports start losing accuracy in detailed data and Google Analytics may display a message telling you the report is based on sampled data, such as:

"This report is based on 100,000 sessions (10.00% of sessions),"

How can data sampling cause issues?

For example, there were 1,000,000 sessions in your selected date range, Google Analytics took 100,000 sessions (10.00% of sessions) to calculate your report metrics and then multiply by 10 to achieve the totals.

Assume Google Analytics has recorded 10,000 sessions for a particular landing page URL from a total of 1,000,000 sessions. This translates to 1% of all sessions for this particular landing page. With 10% sampling, Google Analytics may randomly select any 100,000 sessions from all the 1,000,000 sessions. Within the 100,000 selected sessions, only 8,000 sessions belong to this particular landing page and this is how Google Analytics reports sessions for the particular landing page.

How can data accuracy be improved on sampled data?

In the Google Analytics reports, you have the option to either increase the sample size for improved accuracy, or decrease the sample size for improved report processing speed. All you have to do is to toggle a slider switch.

If you increased the sampled size, your report will be calculated from a larger sample size of sessions. For example:

"This report is based on 200,000 sessions (20.00% of sessions)."

Is the data sampling issue finally resolved?

With the free version of Google Analytics, sampled data cannot be fully avoided, but can be only minimized.

By toggling the slider switch to increase the sampled data size, your reports may improve accuracy. However, Google Analytics has placed limitation on how much sampled data you will get in your reports. i.e. You cannot fully get rid of sampled data in your reports.

What can be done to reduced sampled data?

You want to limit the amount of sampled data showing in your Google Analytics reports.

One of the ways is to reduce the number of unique URLs by:

- Consolidate URLs by converting them into all lower cases.
- Consolidate URLs by using "Exclude URL Query Parameters".
- Use only one URL version for a particular web page.

Consolidate URLs by converting them into all lowercase

Consider the two URLs below.

m.example.com/Hotel/List/Shanghai-Hotels/ m.example.com/hotel/list/shanghai-hotels/

One of the URLs has some capital letters, but the other URL has letters all in lowercase. The web browser returns identical page whether you enter the first URL or the second URL.

However, Google Analytics thinks they are two separate URLs. In Google Analytics, they will show up as two separate rows in reports.

This takes up an additional row in your reports which is really unnecessary. When you have many unnecessary rows in your report, your Google Analytics property will quickly reach the daily upper limit of 50,000 unique rows of pre-aggregated data. Therefore, sampled data will quickly come up in your reports.

You can make them becoming one single row in Google Analytics reports by using filters.

```
View -> Filters -> Add Filter -> Create New Filter
```

- Enter "Lowercase URLs" into the Filter Name field.
- Select the Custom tab, choose Lowercase as the Filter Type, and choose Request URL as the Filter Field.
- Click Save.

The filter converts any capital letters in all URLs into lowercase.

```
m.example.com/hotel/list/shanghai-hotels/
```

Going forward in your Google Analytics reports, you will only see one version of the above URL and it will all be in lowercase.

Consolidate URLs that actually are very similar pages

Consider a hotel booking website which may have a page with URL in which it displays a list of 15 hotels in Shanghai.

```
m.example.com/hotel/list/shanghai
```

Typically for a hotel booking business, you display the hotels that are available for a particular check-in-date and a particular check-out-date. To achieve this, many hotel booking websites would have appended parameters and values to the URLs.

```
m.example.com/hotel/list/shanghai?check-in-date=2015-11-01&check-out-da
te=2015-11-03m.example.com/hotel/list/shanghai?check-in-date=2015-11-05
&check-out-date=2015-11-06
```

The two pages with different check-in and check-out date ranges may have slightly different hotels on each of them, but they are essentially the same page. Having dates as values in your URLs, you can easily end up with an indefinite number of URLs. In many cases, it makes it easier to consider all three URLs as the same page and have them reported as one single URL:

```
m.example.com/hotel/list/shanghai
```

Under your Google Analytics property, go to:

```
View -> View Settings
```

- In the Exclude URL Query Parameters field, enter the name of parameter which needs to be excluded. If you have more than one parameter that need to be excluded, then enter all the names of the parameters separated by commas.
- Note that you should not enter question marks (?), ampersands (&), equals signs (=), or any other symbols or delimiters into the Exclude URL Query Parameters field.
- Now click Save.

In the above case, merging the URLs will reduce the number of unique URLs that are going to appear in your Google Analytics reports. This will result in reducing the data size and give your data more rooms before running into the data sampling issue.

Consolidate URLs that actually mean the same page

Consider this case if your website is using multiple URLs for your home page.

```
m.example.com/m.example.com/index.aspxm.example.com/default.html
```

Practically, you should not be using multiple URLs for a single home page.

- The different versions of URLs sometimes can be confusing to your users.
- In your Google Analytics reports, you always end up with three rows reporting your home page's metrics. This will always take up unnecessary rows in your reports and will get your reports to the row limits quicker than normal circumstances.
- You will have to sum your home page numbers in an unnecessarily clumsy way.

To resolve this, under your Google Analytics property, go to:

```
View -> Filters -> Add Filter -> Create New Filter
```

- Enter "Remove Index and Default" into the Filter Name field.
- Select the Custom tab, choose Search and Replace as the Filter Type, and choose Request URL as the Filter Field.
- For the search string, enter (index|default)\.(aspx|html)
- For the replace string, leave it blank.
- Click Save.

Going forward in your Google Analytics reports, you will end up seeing only one version of URL:

```
m.example.com/
```

Another case with a hotel booking website involves using multiple URL versions of the same page. Consider the list page with 15 hotels in Shanghai. They are two typical ways to represent the same page.

```
Static URL: http://m.example.com/hotel/list/shanghaiDynamic URL:
http://m.example.com/hotel/list?city=shanghai
```

In your Google Analytics reports, you only need one of them to appear, and the better option is the first URL (i.e. the Static URL).

Under your Google Analytics property, go to:

```
View -> Filters -> Add Filter -> Create New Filter
```

- Enter "Remove Index and Default" into the Filter Name field.
- Select the Custom tab, choose Search and Replace as the Filter Type, and choose Request URL as the Filter Field.
- For the search string, enter \?city\=
- For the replace string, V
- Click Save.

Going forward in your Google Analytics reports, you will end up seeing only one version of URL:

```
m.example.com/hotel/list/shanghai
```

If data sampling is a long term problem for your website's data collection, data reporting and data analysis, then consider upgrading to the paid version Google Analytics Premium.

Bad URL consolidation examples

If you make the poor choices to consolidate URLs that should not have been consolidated, then you are going to lose data granularity. Examples of bad choices:

```
m.example.com/hotel/list/shanghaim.example.com/hotel/list/shanghai?dist
rict=xuhui&brand=hantingm.example.com/hotel/list/shanghai?district=chan
gning&brand=jinjiangm.example.com/hotel/list/shanghai?district=baoshan&
brand=hanting
```

All the URLs represent different locations, and it makes no sense to consolidate them into one single URL.

Previous Chapters

- Chapter 13 - Google Analytics Self Referrals

Next Chapters

- Chapter 15 - Google Mobile App Analytics
- Chapter 16 - Google Mobile App Analytics iOS SDK
- Chapter 17 - Google Mobile App Analytics Android SDK

Gordon Choi's Analytics Book has been available since August 2016 and is proudly powered by Folks Analytics.

Google Mobile App Analytics

Chapter 15

The scope of Google mobile app analytics is to track data for mobile apps that are installed on mobile and tablet devices, mainly including those that are running on iOS and Android operating system.

Google Analytics Property Setup

You should setup your Google Analytics account for your mobile apps in the following way.

One Property per App

For example, if you have a pets app and a travel journals app, then each app must be setup on a separate Google Analytics property.

One Property per Operating System

For example, you have a pets app, but in 2 versions. One version is for iOS and the second version is for Android. Setup one Google Analytics property for the iOS app, and a second property for the Android app.

One Property per App Version

For example, you app has been upgraded from version 1.0 to version 2.0. There are obvious and significant differences between the old and the new versions of your app. You will also be expecting almost totally different user behavior on the old version and the new version. It will make sense to setup the apps on two separate Google Analytics properties.

Google Analytics SDKs

Google Analytics tracks your apps through SDKs which are operating system specific (i.e. iOS & Android):

- Google Mobile App Analytics iOS SDK
- Google Mobile App Analytics Android SDK

After implementing the SDKs onto your apps, you will be able to get the following metric data in your Google Analytics reports:

- The number of users
- The number of sessions
- The number of screen views
- Transactions (through Enhance Ecommerce Tracking)

The dimension data which will be available in your Google Analytics reports include:

- Operating systems
- Device related information
- Geographical information

Previous Chapters

Gordon Choi's Analytics Book has been available since August 2016 and is proudly powered by Folks Analytics.

Google Mobile App Analytics iOS SDK

Chapter 16

Let's implement the Google Analytics SDK onto your iOS app.

.xcworkspace

The iOS SDK implementation assumes your app's source code is written in Objective-C and you use CocoaPods to install and manage dependencies.

Open a terminal window and navigate to the location of the Xcode project for your application. Create a Podfile for your application if it doesn't exist.

```
pod init
```

Open the Podfile and add the following:

```
pod 'Google/Analytics'
```

Save the Podfile and run:

```
pod install
```

A .xcworkspace file will be created for your application.

Configuration file

Download the configuration file.

```
https://developers.google.com/mobile/add?platform=ios&cntapi=analytics&
cnturl=https:%2F%2Fdevelopers.google.com%2Fanalytics%2Fdevguides%2Fcoll
ection%2Fios%2Fv3%2Fapp%3Fconfigured%3Dtrue%23add%2Dconfig&cntlbl=Conti
nue%20Adding%20Analytics
```

Drag the GoogleService-Info.plist file (i.e. configuration file) into the root of your Xcode project and add it to all targets.

AppDelegate.m

Add this to the AppDelegate.m file:

```
#import <Google/Analytics.h>
```

To configure GGLContext, override the didFinishLaunchingWithOptions method:

```
NSError *configureError;[[GGLContext sharedInstance]
configureWithError:&configureError];NSAssert(!configureError, @"Error
configuring Google services: %@", configureError);GAI *gai = [GAI
sharedInstance];gai.trackUncaughtExceptions = YES;  // report uncaught
exceptionsgai.logger.logLevel = kGAILogLevelVerbose;  // remove before app
release
```

ViewController.m

Let's add the tracker to track screen views in your iOS View Controller.

In ViewController.m, add the <Google/Analytics.h> header. Use a viewWillAppear method
or function override to insert screen tracking. Give the screen a name and execute
tracking.

```
id<GAITracker> tracker = [[GAI sharedInstance] defaultTracker];[tracker
set:kGAIScreenName value:name];[tracker send:[[GAIDictionaryBuilder
createScreenView] build]];
```

Previous Chapters

- Chapter 15 - Google Mobile App Analytics

Next Chapters

- Chapter 17 - Google Mobile App Analytics Android SDK
- Chapter 18 - Definitions of Metrics & Dimensions
- Chapter 19 - Web Server Log Analytics

Gordon Choi's Analytics Book has been available since August 2016 and is proudly
powered by *Folks Analytics*.

Google Mobile App Analytics Android SDK

Chapter 17

Let's implement the Google Analytics SDK onto your Android app. This Android SDK implementation assumes you use Android Studio and Google Play Services.

AndroidManifest.xml

In your Android app, add INTERNET and ACCESS_NETWORK_STATE permissions to the AndroidManifest.xml file.

```
<manifest xmlns:android="http://schemas.android.com/apk/res/android"
package="com.example.analytics">   <uses-permission
android:name="android.permission.INTERNET"/> <uses-permission
android:name="android.permission.ACCESS_NETWORK_STATE"/>   <application
android:name="AnalyticsApplication">   ... </application></manifest>
```

Build.gradle (Project-level & App-level)

In your Android app, it should have a build.gradle file on the project level, and a second build.gradle file on the app level.

Add the dependency to your project-level build.gradle:

```
classpath 'com.google.gms:google-services:3.0.0'
```

Add the plugin to your app-level build.gradle:

```
apply plugin: 'com.google.gms.google-services'
```

Add the dependency to your app-level build.gradle:

```
compile 'com.google.android.gms:play-services-analytics:9.2.0'
```

Configuration File

Download the google-services.json file (i.e. configuration file). Copy and paste the configuration file onto the app/ directory of your Android Studio project.

```
https://developers.google.com/mobile/add?platform=android&cntapi=analyt
ics&cnturl=https:%2F%2Fdevelopers.google.com%2Fanalytics%2Fdevguides%2F
collection%2Fandroid%2Fv4%2Fapp%3Fconfigured%3Dtrue&cntlbl=Continue%20A
dding%20Analytics
```

AnalyticsApplication.java

Create a new file AnalyticsApplication.java which extends the Application and provides a helper method that returns your application's tracker.

```
package com.google.samples.quickstart.analytics;import
android.app.Application;import
com.google.android.gms.analytics.GoogleAnalytics;import
com.google.android.gms.analytics.Tracker;public class
AnalyticsApplication extends Application {  private Tracker mTracker;
synchronized public Tracker getDefaultTracker() {    if (mTracker == null)
{     GoogleAnalytics analytics = GoogleAnalytics.getInstance(this);
mTracker = analytics.newTracker(R.xml.global_tracker);    }    return
mTracker;  }}
```

MainActivity.java

Let's add the tracking codes to Activities or Fragments of your Android app. The setup allows screen views to be tracked.

In the onCreate method of your activity files (e.g. MainActivity, NextScreenActivity, etc) or the fragment files (e.g. FragmentActivity, etc), add the following:

```
AnalyticsApplication application = (AnalyticsApplication)
getApplication();mTracker = application.getDefaultTracker();
```

In the onResume method of your activity files or onPageSelected of ViewPager, add the following:

```
Log.i(TAG, "Setting screen name: " + name);mTracker.setScreenName("Image~"
+ name);mTracker.send(new HitBuilders.ScreenViewBuilder().build());
```

Add these same codes to all Activities or Fragments which represent "screens".

Previous Chapters

Gordon Choi's Analytics Book has been available since August 2016 and is proudly powered by *Folks Analytics*.

Definitions of Metrics and Dimensions

Chapter 18

Analytics Reports consist of metrics and dimensions.

Metrics (in Analytics)

Metrics are numbers that are used to measure characteristics of dimensions. For example, the characteristics of the Source / Medium dimension may include:

- Sessions
- % New Sessions
- Users
- New Users
- Bounce Rate
- Pages / Session
- Avg. Session Duration
- Goal Conversion Rate
- Goal Completions
- Goal Value

Usually, metrics appear in reports as columns.

Definitions of Basic Analytics Metrics

We'll go through the definitions of the basic analytics metrics including:

- Page Views
- Sessions
- Unique Users
- New Users
- Returning Users
- Page Views / Sessions
- Time on Site
- Bounces & Bounce Rate
- Conversions

Page Views

A page view happens when a user visited one of the web pages on your website. When this user continue visiting a second web page of your website, then the page view count becomes 2. Your website's total page views can be calculated by adding the page view count of all the users.

User	Page Views
User A	5
User B	2
User C	1

User	Page Views
All Users	8

The similar term to page view is unique page view. For example, user A visits your website's page 1, and closes his/her web browser. Then this user repeated this same action 4 more times all within 30 minutes. Note, the user has always only visited the same web page over and over. He/she generated 5 page views through his/her visits, but the unique page view count stays at 1.

User	PV Page 1	PV Page 2	Unique PV
User A	5	0	1
User B	1	1	2
User C	1	0	1
All Users	7	1	4

Sessions

A user visits your website, regardless of how many pages he/she has viewed, and the session count is 1.

We'll go through some examples to demonstrate how sessions are counted. Let's consider the first scenario.

- The user visits one of the pages on your website but doesn't do anything. This counts as 1 session.
- The user keeps his/her web browser open, and has passed 30 minutes of non-activity on your website. His/her session (on your website) expires. Note, by default most web analytics tools expire a session after 30 minutes of a user's non-activity.
- After 30 minutes, the user comes back to his/her web browser, and clicks a link on the page. The user has been taken to the next page, and this starts a new session. This user has generated 2 sessions.

Let's consider the second scenario.

- A user visits your website, clicks and browses several pages. This counts towards 1 session.
- Now the system time of your web analytics tool hits 00h00 which is the next day. The user's session automatically expires.
- The user keeps clicking to view more web pages on your website. This triggers a new session. The total count of this user's sessions is 2.

Note, sessions are sometimes also known as visits.

Unique Users

When a user visits your website for the first time and views one of your web pages, the web analytics tool (installed on your website) sets a new cookie on the user's web browser (e.g. Chrome). The unique user count is 1.

Several hours later this user visits your website again (through Chrome). The web analytics tool remembers this user from the cookie that was set in the first place. The unique user count is still 1.

Still on the same day, the user visits your website through a different web browser (e.g. Firefox). The web analytics tool finds no previous cookie has been set on Firefox, and counts this user as a unique user.

Now your web analytics reports will show 2 unique users, even though it is the same user who has visited your website multiple times on the same day but through different web browsers.

New Users

When a user visits your website for the first time and views one of your web pages, the web analytics tool (installed on your website) sets a new cookie on the user's web browser (e.g. Chrome). The unique user count is 1, and the new user count is 1.

Several hours later this user visits your website again (through Chrome). The web analytics tool remembers this user from the cookie that was set in the first place. The unique user count is still 1, and the new user count is still 1.

Now a second user visits your website for the first time. Your web analytics tool sets a new cookie on the user's web browser (e.g. Firefox). This second user contributes toward a new user.

Now the total new user count (of your website) is 2.

Returning Users

When a user visits your website for the first time and views one of your web pages, the web analytics tool (installed on your website) sets a new cookie on the user's web browser (e.g. Chrome). The unique user count is 1, and the returning user count is 0.

Several hours later this user visits your website again (through Chrome). The web analytics tool remembers this user from the cookie that was set in the first place. The unique user count is still 1, and the returning user count becomes 1.

Page Views / Sessions

Page Views / Sessions is a ratio. Let's demonstrate how we normally use this ratio.

For example, an ecommerce website's page views / sessions on any normal day is between 8 and 9 (e.g. 8.2). This range should become a benchmark for this ecommerce website's user behavior.

After making considerable changes on the website i.e. by cutting down the steps in the purchase funnel for users, on the next day the page views / sessions ratio has become 6.7. When the ratio goes up or goes down more than 1.0, it isn't considered normal. But as long as you understand the reasons behind the ratio change, it is acceptable.

Another example is yesterday the page views / sessions ratio decreases considerably (e.g. from 6.7 to 5.0, i.e. the change is larger than 1.0 again) when they were no critical changes on your website. You may want to look into each major traffic sources' page views / sessions. You may find one suspicious traffic source (e.g. advertising channel X). The day before yesterday, its page views / sessions was 6.0, but all of a sudden yesterday its ratio becomes 1.5. Now you can suspect yesterday advertising channel X has sent your website garbage (or bot) traffic.

Time on Site

Let's explain time on site with an example.

A user visits page A at 21:10:00. He/she visits page B at 21:10:20, and then visits page C at 21:10:50. The user has no further action on your website.

This user's time on page A is calculated by 21:10:20 - 21:10:00 = 20 seconds.

The user's time on page B is 21:10:50 - 21:10:20 = 30 seconds.

But the user's time on page C is unknown. The exact time when the user exits your website altogether (by closing the web browser) is not recorded by your web analytics tool.

The time on site is calculated by time on page A + time of page B = 50 seconds.

Bounces & Bounce Rate

Let's explain bounce and bounce rate with an example.

A bounce happens when a user lands on one of your web pages without any subsequent actions, and then leaves your website (by closing his web browser). Now the bounce count is 1, and session count is 1.

A second users lands on one of your web pages, clicks to open another page on your website. Then he/she leaves your website altogether. This user's bounce count is 0, and session count is 1.

Now your website's bounce count is 1, and session count is 2. Bounce rate is calculated by bounces over sessions.

```
Bounce Rate = (Bounces / Sessions) x 100%
```

So bounce rate is 50%.

Conversions

A conversion is an action that is performed by users on your website.

For example, on a website, registrations can be defined as conversions. Your web analytics tool can be configured to track users' registrations. Your website provides a form for users to fill in their personal details such as name and email address. The user completes and submits the form. He/she is taken to the next page which says "Registration Completes", and now the registration count is 1.

Dimensions (in Analytics)

Dimensions are the attributes of users to your website. For example:

- URLs: Page, landing page, exit page, previous page, hostname, etc.
- Traffic Sources: Source, medium, campaign Keyword, referral path, etc.
- Geography: Country, region, city, etc.
- Devices: Mobile, desktop, tablet, etc.

When a user visits your mobile website, he /she may have the attributes and values below:

- Gender: female
- Age: 35-44
- City: New York
- Source / Medium: Google / Organic
- Keyword: The China Mobile SEO Book
- Browser: Chrome
- Device Category: mobile
- Operating System: Android

Usually, dimensions show up in reports as rows.

Definitions of Basic Analytics Dimensions

We'll go through the definitions of the basic analytics dimensions including:

- Pages
- Landing Pages
- Exit Pages
- Traffic Channels
- Traffic Sources (or Referrers)
- Campaigns
- Keywords

Pages

A page (or web page) is usually the smallest unit of dimension in web analytics. A page is identified as a URL (or web address).

For example, the homepage of domain example.com usually is:

```
www.example.com/ or www.example.com/index.php
```

For example, the category page can be:

```
www.example.com/fruits/ or www.example.com/fruits/index.php
```

The metric page views can be associated with a page. e.g. Web page "A" has 30 page views yesterday.

Landing Pages

A landing page is a web page. For a user's session to your website, a landing page is the entry point for that user, and can be associated with a traffic source (e.g. direct traffic, or Google organic search, or etc).

The metric sessions can be associated with a landing page. e.g. Landing page "A" (m.example.com/fruits/) has 50 sessions yesterday from all traffic sources.

The metric sessions can be associated with a landing page by traffic source. e.g. Landing page "B" (m.example.com/oranges/) has 20 sessions yesterday from direct traffic.

Exit Pages

An exit page is the very last page a user visits before he/she leaves your website (by closing the web browser).

Traffic Channels

A traffic channel is a group of multiple traffic sources all in the same category. The major (and most commonly used) traffic channels are:

- Direct Traffic - Referrer is empty.
- Search Engines (organic search & paid search) - Referrer is a search engine (e.g. Google). The search engine channel is further divided into organic search (e.g. Google organic search) and paid search (e.g. Google paid search).
- Referral Sites - Referrer is a website (e.g. sina.com.cn) but isn't a search engine, and isn't a social media site.
- Social Media Sites - Referrer is a website but is also a social media website (e.g. Facebook).
- Others - When a traffic channel doesn't fit into any of the above.

Traffic Sources (or Referrers)

Traffic sources are the sub-categories of traffic channels. Let's demonstrate with the examples below.

- Google Organic - Google is a search engine, and organic is organic search. Google Organic is a traffic source that falls under the organic search traffic channel.
- Google Paid - Google is a search engine, and paid is paid search. Google Paid is a traffic source that falls under the paid search traffic channel.
- Chinamobileseo.com - For traffic channel, this falls under referral sites. Chinamobileseo.com is the actual traffic source.
- Facebook - For traffic channel, this falls under social media sites. Facbook.com is the actual traffic source.
- Direct Traffic - You will also see direct traffic (or none) reported as one of the traffic sources in your web analytics accounts.

Campaigns

Campaigns are usually used on advertising as a sub-level dimension. For example, under Google paid search you may name a campaign "brand-keywords" and name another campaign "generic-keywords". Another example is Facebook advertising in which you may name a campaign "college-students".

Keywords

Keyword data is usually recorded in your web analytics tools when a user visited your website from a search engine.

Users can come through organic search or paid search. When you have property "tagged" your paid search URLs with keyword data, your keyword data will appear in your web analytics reports for those users who come through paid search.

Users who come through organic search (especially Google or Bing), your web analytics tools may not show any keyword data. This does not mean the users didn't search with any keywords on Google or Bing. Search engines such as Google and Bing in most cases serve search results pages in https protocol, which have restricted the keyword data being passed through to most web analytics tools.

Examples of How Metrics and Dimensions Make Up Reports

For your reports to make any sense, a metric has to be assigned to a dimension. For example, within a specified date range:

- The Mobile device type [dimension] has received 1,000 sessions [metric].
- The Direct traffic [dimension] has been credited with 25 goal conversions [metric].
- The homepage (i.e. /) [dimension] has received 5,000 page views [metric].

Previous Chapters

- Chapter 17 - Google Mobile App Analytics Android SDK

Next Chapters

- Chapter 19 - Web Server Log Analytics
- Chapter 20 - Skills Web Analysts & Mobile App Analysts Must Have
- Chapter 21 - The Big List of Analytics Tools

Gordon Choi's Analytics Book *has been available since August 2016 and is proudly powered by* *Folks Analytics*.

Web Server Log Analytics

Chapter 19

Normally we won't use web server log file data as the main data source to build our analytics reports. But web server log file data can complement what web analytics tools may have lacked.

What's in a Typical Web Server Log File?

The advantage of web server log file data is that it doesn't require tracking pre-installation. Once the web server of your website goes live and is running, it automatically starts recording data.

- When a user visits a page on your website, your web server logs a line of record.
- At the same time when the web page he / she visits has an image, another line of record is logged.

Basically any files that have been triggered to load by a user's visit to your website, the action is recorded in the log file as a line.

Below is a typical log file record in which a user (with IP address 192.168.22.10) visited your website's homepage (/) successfully (i.e. http status 200). The traffic source is www.google.com, and the user was on Firefox when visiting the page.

```
192.168.22.10 - - [21/Nov/2003:11:17:55 -0400] "GET / HTTP/1.1" 200 10801
"http://www.google.com/search?q=china+seo&ie=utf-8&oe=utf-8
&aq=t&rls=org.mozilla:en-US:official&client=firefox-a" "Mozilla/5.0
(Windows; U; Windows NT 5.2; en-US; rv:1.8.1.7) Gecko/20070914
Firefox/2.0.0.7"
```

Issues of Web Server Log Analytics

Log file data has disadvantages.

A full stack analytics reporting system cannot be built from only the data which are collected through web server log files. Most websites nowadays have included JavaScript in which the main purpose is for users to perform interactions on the web pages. Log files aren't able to record any of those JavaScript interactions. This will lead to log file analytics missing a large amount of detailed user interaction (or behavior) data. Note, most typical web analytics tools are able to track JavaScript interactions.

When your website has static file caching enabled (which is what most websites are doing nowadays), the file caching mechanism will serve cached files to "returning" users. For example, images files, CSS files, JavaScript files are all files that are suitable to be cached. When your web server returns cached files to users, the files being served are not recorded in the log file.

A website with daily sessions of 100,000 may generate a web log file that is easily more than 30 gigabytes of pre-processed raw data. That will easily become almost 1 terabyte of raw data per month (or 12 terabytes per year). Processing raw data of such large size into human readable reports everyday can be a difficult and time consuming task. It also takes up a large amount of storage resources (i.e. hard disks) to store the raw data (and the processed data).

Search Engine Spider Data in Web Server Log Files

One major advantage of web server log analytics is search engine spider visits are actually recorded by log files. This is the data typical web analytics aren't able to collect.

Below is a typical log file record when a search engine spider (i.e. Googlebot) visits your website's page (/a.html).

```
66.250.65.101 - - [21/Nov/2003:04:54:20 -0400] "GET /a.html HTTP/1.1" 200
11179 "-" "Mozilla/5.0 (compatible; Googlebot/2.1;
+http://www.google.com/bot.html)"
```

This part of the line reveals the visit was from Googlebot:

```
compatible; Googlebot/2.1; +http://www.google.com/bot.html
```

What We Can Do with Search Engine Spider Data

When dealing with organic search, the traffic funnel is:

```
Crawl -> Index -> Ranking - Traffic
```

Before a search engine can index and rank your web pages, the very first task is to get search engine's spider to crawl your web pages.

Log File Data Reveals Website's Issues

In the log files, whether it is a record of a user's visit, or a record a search engine spider's visit, the record shows a http status code. Below are some of the most frequently seen http status codes.

- 200 – OK
- 301 – Permanently moved
- 302 – Temporarily moved
- 404 – Not found
- 500 – Internal server error
- 503 – Service Unavailable

In the log file, all the records that returns with http status codes 200 or 300 show no issues. All the records which returns with 404, 500 and 503 may have potential issues that will require attention.

Previous Chapters

Next Chapters

Gordon Choi's Analytics Book has been available since August 2016 and is proudly powered by Folks Analytics.

Skills Web Analysts and Mobile App Analysts Must Have

Chapter 20

The Four Tasks

As a web analyst and/or a mobile app analyst, your role requires you to perform four major tasks.

- Perform trend and data reporting.
- Analyze online marketing acquisition strategies and explore new opportunities and/or new strategies.
- Understand on-site (and/or on-app) visitor behavior and experiences.
- Stay connected with the trends and the details.

The Three Phases

In order to accomplish the four major tasks, the web analysts and/or mobile app analysts will actually have to go through three phases.

- Data Collection - Collect and store the raw data which is required for building reports.
- Data Reporting - Process the raw data and have the data presented as analytics reports. The reports can be in table format or graphical format or both.
- Data Analysis - Go through the data reports hoping you will be able to spot data spikes and/or insights for improving your business.

The three phases are traditional phases in analytics (for websites' and mobile apps' data). Let's examine each phase.

Phase 1: Data Collection

Your website's data can be captured through web server log files and/or web analytics tools.

Web Server Log Files

Web server log analytics captures and stores raw data in log files.

Before using log file data as your analytics data, your first set as a web analyst is to ensure your website is correctly configured to capture and store log files.

Web Analytics tools

Most websites use at least one or sometimes multiple web analytics tools.

To enable a web analytics tool to capture your website's basic data, the first step is to implement the required JavaScript based tracking codes onto all pages of your website.

When additional user behavior data is required, you will have to implement some advanced/customized tracking setup.

Mobile App Analytics tools

Most mobile app analytics tools provide SDKs (i.e. SDK for iOS app & SDK for Android app). To enable the mobile app analytics to collect data from your apps, your first step is to install the SDKs onto the mobile apps.

Phase 2: Data Reporting

Once the data is collected, the next phase is to extract the data for the end users. Raw data collected in phase #1 should be converted into reports that are for two major purposes:

- Regular Data Reports
- Ad Hoc Data Reports

Regular Data Reports

These reports need to be received on a regular basis which may be once per day, per week, or per month. These reports are categorized into different levels depending on who the receivers are. An executive (e.g. company CEO) will need high-level reports showing key revenue figures for each major division of the company. Operational managers will need mid-level data reports which allow them to track "potential issues" of the products that individual teams are responsible for.

Ad Hoc Data Reports

These reports won't be processed regularly with any fixed intervals. Normally, ad hoc reports are required for review purposes for any once-off online campaigns. Ad hoc reports are also required when deep diving into data to figure out issues. Issues may be certain KPI numbers have decreased over the past two weeks, and operational managers will need to go through ad hoc data reports in details to figure out the reasons behind the decrease.

Web & Mobile App Analytics tools

Typical web analytics tools and/or mobile app analytics tools provide many basic data reports in user-friendly graphical user interfaces (GUI), and usually the reports can be downloaded as spreadsheets. The pre-built reports allows you to quickly see high-level data trends.

Whether you can perform advanced segmentation and/or compile custom reports, it depends on the specific web / mobile app analytics tool you use. Performing advanced segmentation and/or compiling custom reports allow you to go one (or several) levels deeper into figuring out some real business issues.

Web Server Log Files

With web server log analytics, log files usually are very large files that can be very difficult to process. A mid-size website's daily log file can easily exceed 25 gigabytes in size. You may have to use a third-party log analyzing tool to compile the data into reports.

You must be very familiar with the principles of how web server log files capture data and what data is available. Web server log files give you the ability to "record" all the files that were loaded by the user when they accessed your websites, and you can easily see which "components" of your websites aren't responding to user requests.

Transaction Data and/or Customer Data

Your business intelligence (BI) team may already have captured transaction data and/or customer data and have them stored in a data warehouse software (or multiple databases) e.g. Cognos, Microsoft Reporting Services, etc. At this stage, the transaction data and/or customer data should already been processed into human readable reports.

The next immediate step is to connect the transaction data to your web analytics data and mobile app analytics data. Only after this data connection is established, then your reports will show close to full pictures of your users from how they interact with your website (or mobile apps) to what they have transacted (i.e. purchased).

To build the connection, you may have to use your SQL query writing ability to extract the data directly from the databases (or data warehouse).

Analytics for Advertising Campaign Tracking

If you use one or some of the third-party platforms (e.g. Kenshoo, Marin Software, etc) to track advertising campaigns' performance, then you will have to extract the data and connect it to your web / mobile app analytics data and transaction data.

Phase #3: Data Analysis

Excel & Visualization Reporting Tools

For data analysis, tools such as Excel, and some third-party Visualization reporting tools (e.g. Tableau) are essential.

As an analyst for websites' and mobile apps' data, spending 80% of your time solely on Excel as a tool may be normal. Being able to use the two Excel feature Pivot tables and Vlookup will be important.

R & Python

Tools with steeper learning curves include R, Matlab, and even Python. You may need one or some of them to help you build data models when sophisticated analysis is required.

Next Chapters

Gordon Choi's Analytics Book has been available since August 2016 and is proudly powered by *Folks Analytics*.

The Big List of Analytics Tools

Chapter 21

Analytics tools collect user behavior data from your websites and/or mobile apps, process the collected data and present the data as reports and/or visual reports. Analytics tools consist of different types, including:

- Web analytics
- Mobile app analytics
- Both web & mobile app analytics
- Visual reporting
- Heat / click map analytics
- Big data analytics
- A/B testing analytics
- CRM analytics
- Campaign analytics
- Web server log analytics
- SEO data Analytics

This is the "Big List" of 200+ analytics tools which are currently available in the world.

0-9

123Count	www.123count.com
24Counter	www.24counter.com
51.la	www.51.la
51Yes	count.51yes.com
99Click	www.99click.com

A

AdClarity	www.adclarity.com
AdEmails	www.ademails.com
Adobe Analytics	www.adobe.com
Advanced Web Stats	www.advancedwebstats.com
AFS Analytics	www.afsanalytics.com
Alexa	www.alexa.com
App Adhoc	www.appadhoc.com
App Analytics IO	www.appanalytics.io
App Annie	www.appannie.com
Appsee Mobile	www.appsee.com
Appsflyer	www.appsflyer.com
AT Internet	www.atinternet.com
Aurea Lyris	www.aurea.com
AuriQ Essentia	www.auriq.com
AWeber	www.aweber.com

B

BadgeVille GameViews	www.badgeville.com
Baidu Tongji	tongji.baidu.com
bimeanalytics.com	www.bimeanalytics.com

Bizible	www.bizible.com
BlogCounter	www.blogcounter.com
BunchBall Nitro Analytics	www.bunchball.com

C

Canopy Labs	www.canopylabs.com
Celebrus	www.celebrus.com
Chart.io	www.chart.io
ChartBeat	www.chartbeat.com
ChartMogul	www.chartmogul.com
ClickFox	www.clickfox.com
ClickTale	www.clicktale.com
ClickTracks	www.clicktracks.com
Clicky	www.clicky.com
ClustrMaps	www.clustrmaps.com
CNZZ Tongji	quanjing.cnzz.com
Cobub Razor	www.cobub.com
Cognesia	www.cognesia.com
Compete.com	www.compete.com
comScore Digital Analytix	www.comscore.com
CoreMetrics	welcome.coremetrics.com
Countly	www.count.ly
CQ Counter	www.cqcounter.com
CrazyEgg	www.crazyegg.com
Cross Pixel	www.crosspixel.net
Custora	www.custora.com
Cyfe	www.cyfe.com

D

| Data Fox | www.datafox.com |

Datorama	www.datorama.com
DC Storm	www.dc-storm.com
Decibel Insight	www.decibelinsight.com
Digimind	www.digimind.com

E

Effective Measure	www.effectivemeasure.com
Etracker	www.etracker.com
eVisit Analyst	www.evisitanalyst.com
eXelate (of Nielsen)	www.exelate.com
eXTReMe Tracker	www.extremetracking.com

F

FC2 Analyzer	analyzer.fc2.com
Feedjit	www.feedjit.com
FireBase	firebase.google.com
Flag Counter	www.flagcounter.com
FlightRecorder (ClickTale for Apps)	www.flightrecorder.io
Flurry (of Yahoo)	developer.yahoo.com/analytics/
Folks Analytics	www.folksanalytics.com
Foresee	www.foresee.com
Formisimo	www.formisimo.com

G

GamEffective	www.gameffective.com
Geckoboard	www.geckoboard.com/about
Gemius Heatmap	heatmap.gemius.com
Glew	www.glew.io
GoingUp	www.goingup.com
Gomez	www.ndm.net

Google Analytics	analytics.google.com
GoSquared	www.gosquared.com
GoStats	www.gostats.com
GoStats.cn	www.gostats.cn
Gridsum Web Disector	www.gridsum.com
Growing IO	www.growingio.com
GTopStats	www.gtopstats.com

H

Heap Analytics	www.heapanalytics.com
Heatmaptracker	www.heatmaptracker.com
Histats	www.histats.com
Hit-Counts	www.hit-counts.com
Hits Analytics	www.hitsanalytics.com
HitsLink	www.hitslink.com
HitTail	www.hittail.com
HitWebCounter	www.hitwebcounter.com
Hootsuite	www.hootsuite.com
Hotjar	www.hotjar.com
Hoverowl	www.hoverowl.com
HubSpot	www.hubspot.com/products/analytics

I

IBM Tealeaf	www-01.ibm.com/software/info/tealeaf
IceRocket Blog Tracker	www.icerocket.com
INFOnline	www.infonline.de
Inspectlet	www.inspectlet.com
iWebTrack	www.iwebtrack.com

J

Jirafe	www.jirafe.com
Joojip	www.joojip.com

K

Keen IO	www.keen.io
Kenshoo	www.kenshoo.com
Kick Fire	id.kickfire.com
Kilometer.io	www.kilometer.io
KissMetrics.com	www.kissmetrics.com

L

LabsMedia ClickHeat	www.labsmedia.com/clickheat/
Leadfeeder.com	www.leadfeeder.com
LiveInternet	www.liveinternet.ru
Logaholic	www.logaholic.com
Logdy	www.logdy.com
Looker	www.looker.com
Lotame	www.lotame.com
Lucky Orange	www.luckyorange.com

M

MapMyUser	www.mapmyuser.com
Marin Software	www.marinsoftware.com
Mediametrie	www.mediametrie.com
Mint	www.haveamint.com
MixPanel.com	www.mixpanel.com
MixRank.com	www.mixrank.com
Monetate	www.monetate.com
Mouseflow.com	www.mouseflow.com
Mousestats	www.mousestats.com

MOZ	www.moz.com

N

Navegg	www.navegg.com
Nedstat	www.nedstatpro.net
New Relic	www.newrelic.com
nextSTAT	www.nextstat.com
Numerify	www.numerify.com

O

OneStat	www.onestat.com
Onlinewebstats	www.onlinewebstats.com
Open Web Analytics	www.openwebanalytics.com
Openstat	www.openstat.com
OpenText Optimost	www.optimost.com
Opentracker	www.opentracker.net
Optimizely	www.optimizely.com
Oracle Eloqua	www.oracle.com

P

Parsely	www.parsely.com
Periscope Data	www.periscopedata.com
phpMyVisites	Retired
Pingdom	www.pingdom.com
Piwik	www.piwik.org
pMetrics	pmetrics.performancing.com
PtEngine	www.ptengine.com

Q

Quantcast	www.quantcast.com

Qubit	www.qubit.com
Qubole	www.qubole.com

R

RadarURL	www.radarurl.com
Rambler	www.rambler.ru
RealTracker	www.realtracker.com
Revealytics.com	www.revealytics.com
Revolver Maps	www.revolvermaps.com
RiteCounter	www.ritecount.com
RivalFox.com	www.rivalfox.com

S

SaleForce Radian6	www.salesforce.com
See Volution	www.seevolution.com
Segment	www.segment.com
SEM Rush	www.semrush.com
Sensors Analytics	www.sensorsdata.cn
SEO Book	tools.seobook.com
SessionCam.com	www.sessioncam.com
Shareaholic	www.shareaholic.com
ShinyStat	www.shinystat.com
SimilarWeb	www.similarweb.com
Sisense.com	www.sisense.com
Site Meter	www.sitemeter.com
Siteimprove	www.siteimprove.com
SiteTracker	www.sitetracker.com
Smartlook	www.getsmartlook.com
Snoobi	www.snoobi.fi
SnowPlow	www.snowplowanalytics.com

Splunk	www.splunk.com
Spring Bot	www.springbot.com
Sprout Social	www.sproutsocial.com
stat24	www.stat24.com
Statisfy	www.statisfy.co
Stats Counter	www.statcounter.com
Superfly Insights	insights.superfly.com
Sysomos.com	www.sysomos.com

T

Talking Data	www.talkingdata.com
TechSmith	www.techsmith.com/morae.html
Tencent Analytics	ta.qq.com
Tend	www.tend.io
TraceWatch	www.tracewatch.com
Trackset	www.trackset.com
Tracx.com	www.tracx.com
Trendcounter	www.trendcounter.com

U

Umbel	www.umbel.com
Umeng	www.umeng.com
Unomy	www.unomy.com
Urchin	Retired
Usability Tools	www.usabilitytools.com
UXCam.com	www.uxcam.com

V

None	None

W

W3Counter	www.w3counter.com
Webmasterpro FlashCounter	fc.webmasterpro.de
Weborama	www.weborama.com
Web-Stat	www.web-stat.com
Webtrekk	www.webtrekk.com
WebTrends	www.webtrends.com
Whos.amung.us	whos.amung.us
WiredMinds	www.wiredminds.de
WisePricer	www.wiser.com
Woopra	www.woopra.com
WordPress Stats (Jetpack)	www.jetpack.com
WTStats	www.wtstats.com

X

None	None

Y

Yahoo Web Analytics	Retired
Yandex Metrica	metrica.yandex.com
YoGrow	www.yogrow.co

Z

Zhuge IO	www.zhugeio.com
Zopim	www.zopim.com

Previous Chapters

Next Chapters

Gordon Choi's Analytics Book has been available since August 2016 and is proudly powered by Folks Analytics.

Open Source Web Analytics: Piwik

Chapter 22

Open Source Web Analytics

Most open source web analytics tools were developed by software developers who work on open source development projects. Some of the successfully developed open source web analytics tools include:

- Piwik
- Open Web Analytics (OWA)

Piwik

Piwik is an open source web analytics tool which is free.

Software Installation

Piwik is a pre-built software which can be downloaded from Piwik's official website. You can install the software onto your own Linux Web server or a cloud solution (which provides web servers).

You will have to setup the Piwik Tracking Codes on each page of your website.

Accessing Reports

Piwik has made a few readily built-in reports available. The reports are accessible from within Piwik's user interface.

Storing Data

Each Piwik software comes with a database. The database must be setup to store the website data that will be collected. You will have to manage the regular backup of the database.

Why Using Open Source Web Analytics (i.e. Piwik)

The most conventional alternative to open source web analytics tools is Google Analytics which is the most popular free web analytics tool. You choose Google Analytics mainly because:

- It is free.
- The setup is simple. Most setup requires you adding the Google Analytics JavaScript-based tracking code onto each page on your website.
- You don't want to take care of data storage (i.e the database & the data backup) and the hardware (i.e. the web server, the cloud solution, etc).
- You won't require getting the full set of data onto your own database (for any subsequent detailed data analysis).

Piwik as an open source web analytics tool is also free, but you're going to store the data on your own web servers, and you will have to manage the database (i.e. backup, etc). The major advantage is you get the full set of your website's data on Piwik's database, and you will be able to make use of this data for any subsequent detailed data analysis.

Gordon Choi's Analytics Book has been available since August 2016 and is proudly powered by Folks Analytics.

Piwik Tracking Codes

Chapter 23

Piwik uses a JavaScript-based tracking code to track website's data. The tracking code must be placed on each page of a website for Piwik to start tracking the website's data.

Piwik JavaScript-based Tracking Code

After completing your Piwik software's installation, log onto Piwik from your web browser. Your Piwik's login page URL should be located at:

```
data.example.com/piwik/piwik.php
```

Follow the below path to get your Piwik Tracking Code.

```
Settings -> Websites -> View Tracking Code
```

To track your website's data, add the following Piwik tracking code onto each page of your website. This tracking code is for default Piwik setup.

```
<script type="text/javascript">var _paq = _paq ||
[];_paq.push(['trackPageView']);_paq.push(['enableLinkTracking']);(func
tion() {var u="//data.example.com/piwik/";_paq.push(['setTrackerUrl',
u+'piwik.php']);_paq.push(['setSiteId', '1']);var d=document,
g=d.createElement('script'),
s=d.getElementsByTagName('script')[0];g.type='text/javascript';
g.async=true; g.defer=true; g.src=u+'piwik.js';
s.parentNode.insertBefore(g,s);})();</script>
```

The web server in which your Piwik software has been installed has a URL. The 2 lines below specifies the location of the URL.

```
var u="//data.example.com/piwik/";_paq.push(['setTrackerUrl',
u+'piwik.php']);
```

Each website you created in your Piwik account has a unique site ID. This specific website has a siteID = 1.

```
_paq.push(['setSiteId', '1']);
```

The line sends the data to Piwik as a page view.

```
_paq.push(['trackPageView']);
```

If your Piwik's web server URL may have been installed on a "https" protocol, then evaluate the protocol type using this function:

```
(function(){ var u=(("https:" ==
document.location.protocol) ?"https://data.example.com/piwik/" :
"http://data.example.com/piwik/");...}
```

The updated tracking code will become:

```
<script type="text/javascript">var _paq = _paq ||
[];_paq.push(['trackPageView']);_paq.push(['enableLinkTracking']);(func
tion(){ var u=(("https:" ==
document.location.protocol) ?"https://data.example.com/piwik/" :
"http://data.example.com/piwik/");_paq.push(['setTrackerUrl',
u+'piwik.php']);_paq.push(['setSiteId', '1']);var d=document,
g=d.createElement('script'),
s=d.getElementsByTagName('script')[0];g.type='text/javascript';
g.async=true; g.defer=true; g.src=u+'piwik.js';
s.parentNode.insertBefore(g,s);})();</script>
```

Piwik's JavaScript-based tracking code is asynchronous. Asynchronous means the tracking code can execute in the background without blocking other scripts and content of your website. This allows the visible layout of your web page's to load and appear to your users faster. Faster web page loading means better user experience.

Piwik Goal Tracking

As an example, let's demonstrate how to create a new goal for tracking your website's registrations.

- While on Piwik's Dashboard, click "Goals".
- Enter a goal name in the "Goal Name" field.
- Under "Goal is trigger", select "when visitors" and select the "Visit a given URL" radio button.
- Under "where the Page Title", select "contains" and enter the URL path when a registration completes. e.g. /registration/success.php
- Click "Add Goal".

Piwik Campaign Tracking

To track your campaign's performance with Piwik, you will have to tag your campaign advertising URLs with a parameter:

```
pk_campaign
```

For example, your display advertising campaign's URL may become:

```
http://www.example.com/promo.php?pk_campaign=my-email-promo-nov-2016
```

For paid search campaigns in which you will need to track keywords, tag your URLs with an additional parameter:

```
pk_campaignpk_keyword
```

For example, your Baidu paid search campaign's URL may become:

```
http://www.example.com/book.php?pk_campaign=baidu_ppc_tcmsb-brand&pk_kw
d=the-china-mobile-seo-book
```

If your website is using Google Analytics and Piwik at the same time, you may have to explicitly tag both sets of parameters to your URL i.e. One set of parameters for Google Analytics and a second set of parameters for Piwik).

```
http://www.example.com/book.php?pk_campaign=baidu_ppc_tcmsb-brand&pk_kw
d=the-china-mobile-seo-book&utm_source=baidu&utm_medium=cpc&utm_campaig
n=tcmsb-brand&utm_term=the-china-mobile-seo-book
```

Another tip is: Piwik is able to recognize the two Google Analytics parameters below:

```
utm_campaignutm_keyword
```

Because Piwik understands the two Google Analytics parameters, it can recognize the two URL tagging below are identical. For the second URL, the value in utm_campaign will show up under Piwik's campaign report as campaign names. The value in utm_term will show up under the keyword report.

```
http://www.example.com/book.php?pk_campaign=baidu_ppc_tcmsb-brand&pk_kw
d=the-china-mobile-seo-bookhttp://www.example.com/book.php?utm_campaign
=baidu_ppc_tcmsb-brand&utm_kwd=the-china-mobile-seo-book
```

Piwik Ecommerce Tracking

For ecommerce websites, Piwik is able to track ecommerce transactions. For Piwik ecommerce tracking to work, additional JavaScript codes regarding the transactions must be added to the "purchase confirmation" page.

To track an "item" (of a transaction) that are purchased:

```
_paq.push(['addEcommerceItem',"sku0129303", // SKU (Compulsory)"XYZ Fruit
Juice", // Product Item Name (Compulsory)"Food/Imported/Juice", // Category
(Optional)10.00, // Unit Price (Compulsory)12 // Quantity (Compulsory)]);
```

All items must be included in a transaction (i.e. order):

```
_paq.push(['trackEcommerceOrder',"R0000001", // Order ID
(Compulsory)185.00, // Total (Compulsory)180.00, // Subtotal (Optional)0.0,
// Tax (Optional)5.0, // Shipping Fee (Optional)false // Discount (false
is no discount)]);
```

Below is the full Piwik tracking code which should be triggered on the purchase confirmation page. Note, the ecommerce tracking code has included 2 items in a single transaction (or order).

```
<script type="text/javascript">var _paq = _paq || [];(function() {var
u="//data.example.com/piwik/";_paq.push(['setTrackerUrl',
u+'piwik.php']);_paq.push(['setSiteId',
'1']);_paq.push(['addEcommerceItem',"sku0129303", // SKU (Compulsory)"XYZ
```

```
Fruit Juice", // Product Item Name (Compulsory)"Food/Imported/Juice", //
Category (Optional)10.00, // Unit Price (Compulsory)12 // Quantity
(Compulsory)]);_paq.push(['addEcommerceItem',"sku0617172", // SKU
(Compulsory)"Sunny Yogurt", // Product Item Name
(Compulsory)"Food/Domestic/Refrigerated", // Category (Optional)30.00, //
Unit Price (Compulsory)2 // Quantity
(Compulsory)]);_paq.push(['trackEcommerceOrder',"R0000001", // Order ID
(Compulsory)185.00, // Total (Compulsory)180.00, // Subtotal (Optional)0.0,
// Tax (Optional)5.0, // Shipping Fee (Optional)false // Discount (false
is no
discount)]);_paq.push(['trackPageView']);_paq.push(['enableLinkTracking
']);var d=document, g=d.createElement('script'),
s=d.getElementsByTagName('script')[0];g.type='text/javascript';
g.async=true; g.defer=true; g.src=u+'piwik.js';
s.parentNode.insertBefore(g,s);})();</script>
```

Piwik Event Tracking

With Piwik, you are able to track user actions such as a button click. The "trackEvent"
function allows tracking of events including button clicks, and has the format below.

```
trackEvent(category, action, [name], [value])
```

The compulsory parameters are:

```
categoryaction
```

The optional parameters are:

```
[name][values]
```

As an example, you are to implement a "click event" for the side menu button that reads
"Fruits". You will use trackEvent function in this format:

```
_paq.push(['trackEvent', 'SideMenu', 'Click', 'Fruits']);
```

On the actual button of your web page, you may include the trackEvent function within the
"onclick" attribute in an <a href> tag.

```
<a href="http://www.example.com/fruits/"
onclick="javascript:_paq.push(['trackEvent', 'SideMenu',
'Fruits']);">Freedom page</a>
```

Piwik Custom Variables

A custom variable consists of an index, a name, a value and its scope. Piwik lets you track if a user visits a specific page URL and record the user's information.

Piwik's custom variable takes the following format:

```
setCustomVariable(index, name, value, scope)
```

As an example, let's track the member IDs of the registration members who have logged-on while visiting your website. The setCustomVariable function sets the custom variable index to 1, the name to 'logged-on', the value to the member's ID (i.e. id002931), and the scope to 'visit'.

```
_paq.push(['setCustomVariable', 1, 'logged-on', 'id002931', 'visit']);
```

The "if-statement" checks if a user has visited the "member area" page (which means the user has logged on). If a user has logged on, then the setCustomVariable function will send the member ID to Piwik's database.

```
if (location.pathname.toLowerCase() ==
"/member-area/"){ _paq.push(['setCustomVariable', 1, 'logged-on',
'id002931', 'visit']);}
```

Note, Piwik allows using a maximum of 5 custom variables.

Previous Chapters

- Chapter 22 - Open Source Web Analytics: Piwik

Next Chapters

- Chapter 24 - Piwik Performance Optimization

Piwik Performance Optimization

Chapter 24

First ensure your server has the minimum requirements for running Piwik. Then consider optimizing your Piwik setup's performance.

Piwik's Minimum Requirements

Check on your web server that it meets the minimum requirements for running Piwik.

- Your web server is running Nginx.
- PHP version 5.3.3 or greater has been installed.
- MySQL version 4.1 or greater, or MariaDB has been installed.
- The PHP extension pdo and pdo_mysql, or the mysqli extension has been installed.

Note, the minimum requirements listed above may change in time when the Piwik software gets new upgrades in the future.

Optimize Piwik's Performance

To optimize your Piwik setup's performance, consider the items below.

- Server & RAM (hardware)
- Load Balancers
- Real-time Reports
- Number of Unique URLs
- PHP Caching
- Crontab

Server & RAM

This method will require investing additional budget into your Piwik setup. You use a better (or upgrade) your server (i.e. your machine, or main hardware).

The best you can get is to run Piwik on a completely dedicated server, which is shared with no other software that isn't required by your Piwik setup.

Most cloud solutions are a good option. Cloud solutions allows flexibility for upgrading your hardware (i.e. server, RAM, CPU, hard disk space, etc).

Load Balancers

Using a load balancer means your Piwik setup is using multiple servers. A load balancer can evenly distribute your Piwik setup's workload across multiple servers.

- When using load balancers, you may end up having multiple config.ini.php files across multiple servers. Use rsync to synchronous all the config.ini.php files.
- In Piwik's config.ini.php file, enable SSL by ading "force_ssl=1" under the [General] section.
- Enable database session storage in Piwik's config.ini.php file by assigning "dbtable" to variable "session_save_handler".
- Each time after upgrading the Piwik software (or any plugins), remove tmp/* folder's content.

Adding load balancers and/or additional servers also require investing additional budget to your Piwik setup.

Report Processing Interval

By default, Piwik's report processing interval may have been set to 150 seconds. To make Piwik runs more smoothly, increase the interval to 3600 seconds (i.e. 60 minutes or 1 hour) or even 7200 seconds (120 minutes or 2 hours). To set it, go to:

```
Administration -> General -> Archive reports at most every X seconds
```

Enter a larger value (such as 3600 or 7200) in the "seconds" field.

Number of Unique URLs

The more unique URLs Piwik has to track, the more data Piwik has to store in the database, and the quicker Piwik's database becomes larger in size. By keeping the database size smaller in a logical way, it prevents Piwik's performance from going down quickly.

In theory all pages below refer to pages with highly similar content (or sometimes even identical pages).

```
www.example.com/hotels/list-shanghai/www.example.com/hotels/list-shangh
ai/?checkin-date=2016-03-01&checkout-date=2016-03-02www.example.com/hot
els/list-shanghai/?checkin-date=2016-05-15&checkout-date=2016-05-18
```

They are only differ on the URL by the tagged parameters.

```
checkin-date=2016-03-01&checkout-date=2016-03-02checkin-date=2016-05-15
&checkout-date=2016-05-18
```

You may exclude the URLs when storing the URLs in Piwik's database. Go to:

```
Administration -> Websites -> Global list of Query URL parameters to exclude
```

Enter the list of URL Query Parameters, one per line.

Note, one or more URL parameters are specified for exclusion, it will only affect data
going forward, and URL parameters will not be removed from your historical data and
reports in retrospect.

PHP Caching

Optimize your Piwik's PHP codes by using a PHP cache (e.g. XCache).

Crontab

By default, Piwik triggers the report archiving process whenever you log onto Piwik's
account interface through a web browser. If your website has relatively high number of
user sessions per day, then waiting for Piwik to archive your data may take several
minutes or even more. To avoid the waiting times, set up a cron job on your Linux server
to have your data automatically processed every hour.

To automatically trigger the Piwik archives, you can set up a script that will execute every
hour. On your Piwik's Linux machine, you will set up a Crontab to automatically archive
your Piwik reports. A crontab is a time-based scheduling service in a Linux server, and
requires php-cli or php-cgi installed. You will also need SSH access to your server in order
to set it up.

Create a new crontab with the text editor nano:

```
nano /etc/cron.d/piwik-archive
```

Add the lines to the crontab:

```
MAILTO="youremail@example.com"5 * * * * www-data /usr/bin/php5
/path/to/piwik/console core:archive --url=http://example.org/piwik/ >
/home/example/piwik-archive.log
```

The Piwik archive script will run every hour (at 5 minutes past). Normally the script should complete in 1 minute to 30 minutes depending on the amount of traffic your website is getting.

Let's examine the content of the crontab. If there is an error during the script execution, the script output and error messages will be sent to the youremail@example.com address.

```
MAILTO="youremail@example.com"
```

This is the user that the cron job will be executed by, and it should generally be your web server user.

```
www-data
```

This is the path to your PHP executable. The path may vary depending on your server configuration and operating system. To find out the the path of your PHP5 executable, execute the command "which php5" or "which php" in a Linux shell.

```
/usr/bin/php5
```

Below is the only required parameter in the script, which must be set to your Piwik base URL eg. http://analytics.example.org/ or http://example.org/piwik/

```
%%--url=http://example.org/piwik/%%
```

Below is the path where the script will write the output. You can replace this path with /dev/null if you prefer not to log the last piwik cron output text. The script output contains useful information such as which websites are archived, how long it takes to process for each date & website, etc.

```
/home/example/piwik-archive.log
```

Below is the optional path where the script will write the error messages. If you omit this from the cron tab, then errors will be emailed to your MAILTO address. If you write this in the crontab, then errors will be logged in this specified error log file.

```
/home/example/piwik-archive-errors.log
```

The cron utility uses two different types of configuration files:

- System crontab
- User crontab

The only difference between the two different types of configuration files is the sixth field.

In the system crontab, the sixth field is the name of a user for the command to run as. This gives the system crontab the ability to run commands as any user.

In a user crontab, the sixth field is the command to run, and all commands run as the user who created the crontab. This is a security feature.

If you set up your crontab as a user crontab, you will have to write:

```
5 * * * * /usr/bin/php5 /path/to/piwik/console core:archive
--url=http://example.org/piwik/ > /dev/null
```

This cron job will trigger the day/week/month/year archiving process at 5 minutes past every hour. This will make sure that when you visit your Piwik's account interface, the data has already been processed. Your Piwik reports should load as normal.

You can test the cron command. Make sure the crontab will actually work by running the script as the crontab user in the shell:

```
su www-data -c "/usr/bin/php5 /path/to/piwik/console core:archive
--url=http://example.org/piwik/"
```

You should see the script output with the list of websites being archived, and a summary at the end stating that there was no error.

Previous Chapters

Gordon Choi's Analytics Book has been available since August 2016 and is proudly powered by *Folks Analytics*.